ROUTLEDGE LIBRARY EDITIONS: GERMAN HISTORY

I0130669

Volume 13

FROM KAISERREICH TO THIRD REICH

FROM KAISERREICH TO THIRD REICH

Elements of Continuity in German History
1871–1945

FRITZ FISCHER
TRANSLATED AND WITH AN INTRODUCTION
BY ROGER FLETCHER

Routledge
Taylor & Francis Group

NEW YORK AND LONDON

First published in English in 1986 by George Allen & Unwin Ltd

This edition first published in 2020
by Routledge
52 Vanderbilt Avenue, New York, NY 10017

and by Routledge
2 Park Square, Milton Park, Abingdon, Oxon OX14 4RN

Routledge is an imprint of the Taylor & Francis Group, an informa business

British Library Cataloguing in Publication Data
A catalogue record for this book is available from the British Library

ISBN: 978-0-367-02813-8 (Set)
ISBN: 978-0-429-27806-8 (Set) (ebk)
ISBN: 978-0-367-23592-5 (Volume 13) (hbk)
ISBN: 978-0-367-23616-8 (Volume 13) (pbk)
ISBN: 978-0-429-28077-1 (Volume 13) (ebk)

Publisher's Note
The publisher has gone to great lengths to ensure the quality of this reprint but points out that some imperfections in the original copies may be apparent.

Disclaimer
The publisher has made every effort to trace copyright holders and would welcome correspondence from those they have been unable to trace.

From Kaiserreich to Third Reich

Elements of Continuity in German History, 1871–1945

Fritz Fischer

Translated and with an Introduction by

Roger Fletcher

ROUTLEDGE

London and New York

Originally published in German under the title Fritz Fischer,
Bündnis der Eliten
© 1979 by Droste Verlag GmbH, Düsseldorf.

This translation first published in 1986
Third impression 1990

Reprinted in 1991 by
Routledge
11 New Fetter Lane, London EC4P 4EE
29 West 35th Street, New York NY 10001

British Library Cataloguing in Publication Data

Fischer, Fritz
 From Kaiserreich to Third Reich: elements
 of continuity in German history, 1871–1945.
1. Germany–History–1871–1918
2. Germany–History–20th century
I. Title   II. Bündnis der Eliten. *English*
943.08   DD220
ISBN 0-415-07878-4

Library of Congress Cataloging-in-Publication Data

Fischer, Fritz
 From Kaiserreich to Third Reich.
Translation of: Bündnis der Eliten.
Bibliography: p.
Includes index.
1. Germany – Politics and government – 1871–1933 –
Addresses, essays, lectures. 2. Germany – Politics,
and government – 1933–1945 – Addresses, essays, lectures.
3. Elite (Social sciences) – Germany – History. I. Title.
JN3388.F5713 . 1986   943.08   85–32065
ISBN 0-415-07878-4

Set in 11 on 12½ point Garamond by Paston Press, Norwich
and printed in Great Britain by Billing and Sons Ltd,
London and Worcester

Contents

Acknowledgements

Thanks are due to several persons and institutions for their assistance in the preparation of this book: to Ray Duplain of Deakin University, Australia, for drawing the maps; to Carolyn and Lisa, who did most of the typing; to John Moses, for useful suggestions regarding the translation; to Hazel Blumberg-McKee, for the indexing; to Tim McMullin and the editors of *Teaching History*, for permission to use, in the introduction, some of the material and ideas which first appeared in 'Germany and the 1914 Question: An Epilogue to the Fischer Thesis' (in volume 18, number 4 of this journal). The publishers, Chatto and Windus, of London, UK and W. W. Norton, of New York, USA, have kindly agreed to the use, again in the introduction, of a rather long extract from Professor Fischer's *Germany's Aims in the First World War*, and for this, too, we are most grateful.

Territories considered for direct membership

Countries considered for association

Territories designated for annexation in 1916

Territories considered for incorporation after the collapse of the western offensive

Territories considered for close political and economic association with Germany after the peace of Brest-Litovsk and Berlin

0 100 200 300 km

NORWAY
Christiania
SWEDEN
FINLAND
Helsinki
St Petersburg
ESTONIA
LIVONIA
Riga
COURLAND
Mitau
LITHUANIA
Vilna
Brest-Litovsk
RUSSIA
BALTIC SEA
NORTH SEA
DENMARK
Copenhagen
Berlin
GERMANY
Warsaw
POLAND
NETHERLANDS
Brussels
BELGIUM
LUXEMBOURG
Bern
SWITZERLAND
FRANCE
Paris
GREAT BRITAIN
London
ATLANTIC OCEAN
PORTUGAL
Lisbon
SPAIN
Madrid
Corsica
Sardinia
Rome
ITALY
Vienna
AUSTRIA-HUNGARY
Belgrade
Dalmatia
SERBIA
MONTENEGRO
ALBANIA
Valona
GREECE
BULGARIA
RUMANIA
Bucharest
BLACK SEA
Constantinople
TURKEY
MEDITERRANEAN SEA

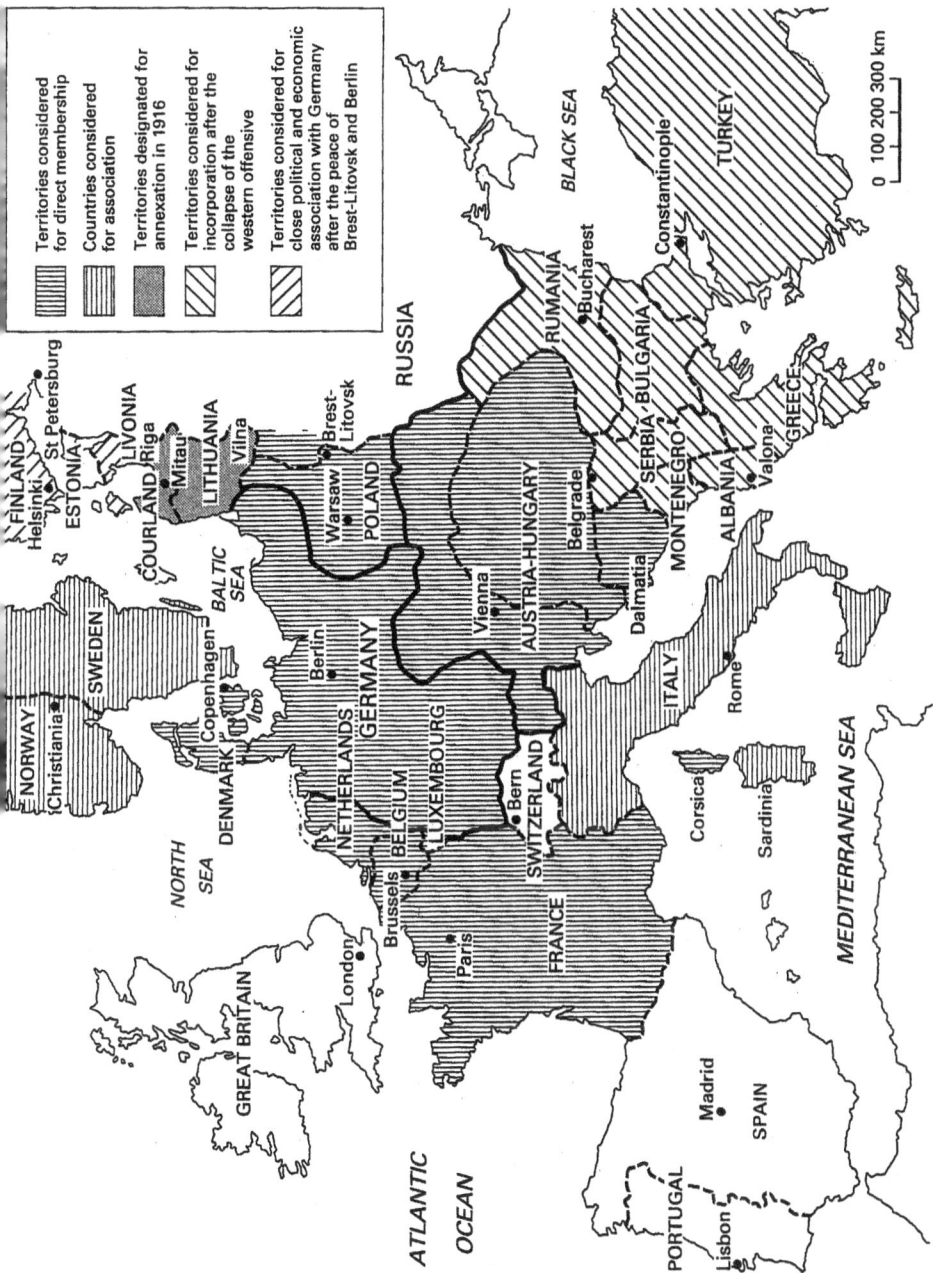

Map 1 'Central Europe' as a new economic unit. Conception of the middle European tariff union in Bethmann Hollweg's programme of September 1914

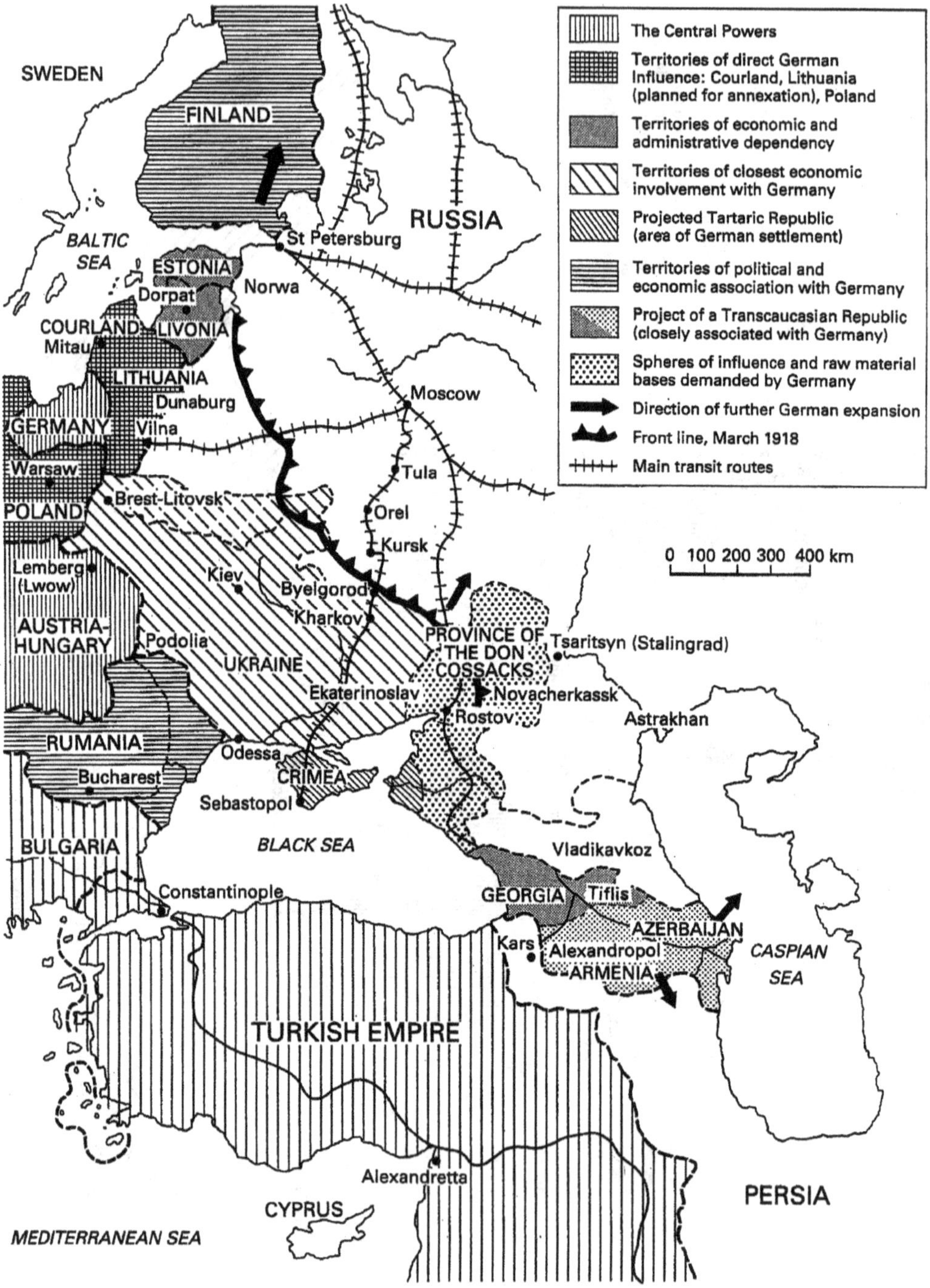

Map 2 The 'New Order' in the East, 1914–1918

Legend:

- ||||| The Central Powers
- Territories of direct German Influence: Courland, Lithuania (planned for annexation), Poland
- Territories of economic and administrative dependency
- Territories of closest economic involvement with Germany
- Projected Tartaric Republic (area of German settlement)
- Territories of political and economic association with Germany
- Project of a Transcaucasian Republic (closely associated with Germany)
- Spheres of influence and raw material bases demanded by Germany
- → Direction of further German expansion
- ▲▲▲ Front line, March 1918
- +++++ Main transit routes

0 100 200 300 400 km

Map labels:

SWEDEN

FINLAND

RUSSIA

BALTIC SEA

St Petersburg

ESTONIA
Dorpat   Norwa

COURLAND LIVONIA
Mitau

Moscow

LITHUANIA
Dunaburg

GERMANY
Vilna

Tula

Warsaw

Brest-Litovsk

POLAND

Orel

Lemberg (Lwow)   Kiev   Byelgorod   Kursk

Kharkov

AUSTRIA-HUNGARY   Podolia

UKRAINE

PROVINCE OF THE DON COSSACKS   Tsaritsyn (Stalingrad)

Ekaterinoslav   Novacherkassk

Rostov   Astrakhan

RUMANIA

Odessa

CRIMEA

Bucharest

Sebastopol

BLACK SEA

Vladikavkoz

BULGARIA

Constantinople

GEORGIA   Tiflis

AZERBAIJAN

Kars   Alexandropol

CASPIAN SEA

ARMENIA

TURKISH EMPIRE

PERSIA

Alexandretta

CYPRUS

MEDITERRANEAN SEA

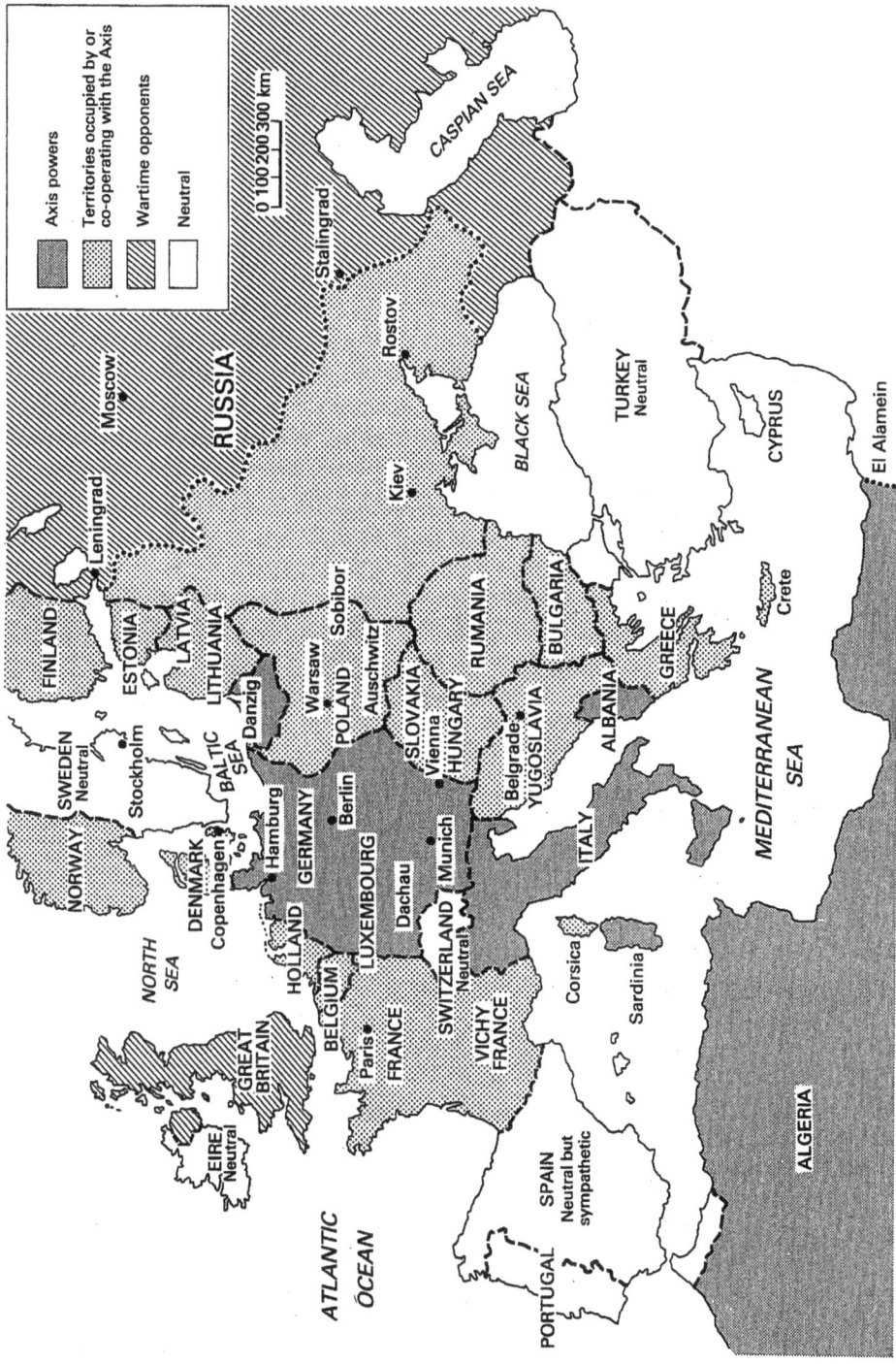

Map 3 The Third Reich at its greatest extent, 1942

Introduction

Reviewing Barrington Moore, Jr's, *Injustice: The Social Basis of Obedience and Revolt*, Guenther Roth expressed the truism that 'it is always risky for a scholar to write a sum of his knowledge and insights toward the end of his career.'[1] This, in effect, is what Fritz Fischer has done in the present book. Never noted as one for shirking risks, Professor Fischer here offers the Anglo-American reader a concise articulation of his empirical findings and a clear application of the Fischer methodology, all within the framework of an explicitly stated pedagogic purpose.

Fischer's most obvious contribution to modern German historiography lies in his attempt to provide a number of challenging insights into, and controversial reinterpretations of, the recent German past. In particular, it is now widely recognized that 'Fritz Fischer's work . . . [has] had a major impact on interpretation' of the origins and nature of the First World War,[2] but in 1961 he burst like a bomb-shell on the staid West German historical scene with a book entitled *Griff nach der Weltmacht (Grasp at World Power)*, arguing that the Kaiser's Germany, no less than Hitler's Reich, had aimed at empire in the grand manner:

A survey of Germany's aims at the beginning and in the middle of 1918, when German self-confidence was at its peak in the expectation of early victory, discloses a picture of an *imperium* of grandiose dimensions. In the west: Belgium, Luxemburg, Longwy-Briey linked with Germany on such terms as to make possible the adherence of France and Holland and to isolate Britain and force her to recognise Germany's position; in the east: Courland, Livonia, Estonia and Lithuania, from Reval to Riga and Vilno, the Polish Frontier Strip and Rump Poland all closely fettered to Germany; in the south-east: Austria-Hungary clamped into

1

Germany as a corner-stone, then Rumania and Bulgaria, and beyond them the Ottoman Empire as an object of Germany's Asiatic policy. Command of the eastern Mediterranean was to compel the adherence of Greece and secure the route through Suez, while the domination of the Black Sea guaranteed the economic mastery of the Ukraine, the Crimea and Georgia, and the command of the Baltic compelled Sweden and Finland, with their riches, to take the German side. On top of all this was the position of at least economic hegemony in Rump Russia.

The counterpart overseas of this European extended basis – Mitteleuropa surrounded by a ring of vassal states – was to be the central African colonial empire safeguarded by naval bases and linked with the Near East through the Sudan and Suez. With this economic and political power in Africa, reinforced by the command of the strategic and technical key-points on the route to South America to expand and consolidate the strong economic interests already established there before the war, Germany was to make herself a colonial and economic power of world status. Yet concentration on the African empire implied no withdrawal from the eastern hemisphere. Germany was maintaining her interests in Samoa and New Guinea and trying to initiate in China a more elastic policy, confined purely to the safeguarding of her economic interests. Above all, she hoped that by ceding Kiaochow to Japan she would be able to renew her old connections with that country against both Russia and the Anglo-Saxon powers.

Germany's political and economic *imperium* would have represented a concentration of force far surpassing Bismarck's empire in resources and human material. The old industrial areas of the Ruhr and Luxemburg, the Saar, German Lorraine, Saxony and Upper Silesia were to be reinforced by French Lorraine, Belgium, Poland and Bohemia. For her supply of ore, besides her own production and the assured imports from Sweden, she could have drawn on the ores of Austria, Poland, Longwy-Briey, the Ukraine, the Caucasus, Turkey and Katanga. To the oil of Galicia was added that of Rumania, the Caucasus and Mesopotamia, to her own agricultural production that of the Balkans and the north-east, to her previous imports from her old colonies in Africa, the abundant produce of central Africa; markets previously contested would be replaced by near-monopoly in Georgia, Turkey, Russia, the Ukraine, the Balkans, the north-east, the north and the west. The weight of the German Reich in matters of commercial policy would unquestionably have put Germany in an impregnable position of world-economic power. The economic agreements were, moreover, to be safeguarded by military treaties.

Military conventions with Finland, the Baltic states, Lithuania, Poland, the Ukraine, Georgia, Turkey, Bulgaria, Rumania and Austria-Hungary, and in a negative sense also with Belgium, had been planned, and most of them at least initialled. Through these economic, political and military links Germany would have created a European bloc which would have put her on a level with the three world powers of America, Britain and – if she could still be counted – Russia, and have given her a rank far above that of any European power of the old days.[3]

In this thoroughly researched and extensively documented book, Fischer insisted that German war aims during the First World War had to be viewed as a logical outcome of German prewar policy, including German policy during the July crisis of 1914; that these war aims were offensive and designed to establish an overt German hegemony on the European Continent, as well as to guarantee the realization of a German superpower position of epochal dimensions; and that the aggressively expansionist character of German war-aims policies, far from being the work of particular personalities, could be fully understood only when comprehended as part of the old ruling elites' determination to preserve their own dominance within the society and politics of Imperial Germany.[4]

While endeavouring to rebut his many critics, Fischer produced a second monumental tome, entitled *Krieg der Illusionen* (1969).[5] Here he sought to demonstrate that German prewar policy had been dominated by the same objectives as were pursued by Germany during the First World War. At the same time, he argued that the pursuit of these objectives – though by no means the sole cause of the First World War – represented the one factor which rendered inevitable the outbreak of global war in August 1914. Here the roots of Wilhelmine imperialism were located in the prevailing climate of ideas (with its deep cultural pessimism, its sense of mission, its novel, global and geopolitical conception of imperialism, as well as its rabid Russophobia), in the acute social tensions created, in particular, by Germany's exceptionally rapid modernization (evoking a social-imperialist response) and in Germany's position as an imperial latecomer (encouraging, *inter alia*, neo-mercantilist proclivities). Conditioned by such forces, structures and assumptions, the dominant elites of Junker-dom and big business, together with the official leaders of Wilhelmine Germany, who spoke on behalf of these elites, succumbed to the illusion that the one sure solution to their class and national difficulties lay in the conversion of the Bismarckian nation-state into a Greater Germanic superpower or world empire. Beginning with Bismarck – and certainly no later than the close of the 1890s – the antediluvian hegemons of German business and polit-ical life consistently pursued expansionist objectives *both* on the European Continent (*Mitteleuropa*, with its Berlin to Baghdad projection) *and* overseas (a consolidated German Central African Empire, or *Mittelafrika*, being the jewel in this crown). Pre-1914 German imperialists naturally differed as to priorities – some advocated *Weltpolitik*, which gave pre-eminence to the Tirpitz battleship navy against Britain, while others attached supreme importance to Continental expansion and therefore gave prece-dence to the army – but all were convinced that the German nation stood at the crossroads: either Germany effected a break-through to superpower status or she faced inevitable, rapid and irreversible decline. All German imperialists recognized that the pursuit of world empire entailed both Continental and overseas expansion as well as acceptance of the risk of a major war.

The methods employed by successive German governments in the Wilhelmine era included the policy of the 'free hand' (economic and political autarchy) and the cultivation of British amity, which was designed to realize, as an absolute minimum, *de facto* British neutrality in the event of a Franco-German 'settlement of accounts' – at least during the crucial early phase of the anticipated conflict. In Fischer's view, these were the constants in German foreign policy from Bismarck through to Bethmann Hollweg and beyond. The variables employed in the pursuit of Wilhelmine imperialist ambitions included the Continental bloc idea (essentially, an agreement with Russia) and the use of the threat of war (most notably applied against France in 1905 and 1911, and against Russia in 1909). Until 1911, however, very little had been achieved. The gap between aspiration and accomplishment remained, in the eyes of the German ruling classes, as frustratingly wide as ever, for one and a half decades of 'world policy' had yielded no substantial gains. In fact, 'world empire' seemed as much a mirage in 1911–12 as it had done in 1897.

After 1911, German imperialism was perceived as having entered a state of acute crisis. Not only had Germany failed to achieve the desired breakthrough to superpower status, but she had now to contemplate, thanks to the successful 'encirclement' response of the Triple Entente, the prospect of the imminent blocking-off of all avenues to future expansion. Because of Germany's worsening economic position (French resistance to the *'pénétration pacifique'* of German industry in the iron-ore regions of Lorraine and Normandy; the clash with Russian vital interests at Constantinople and the Straits in the Liman von Sanders mission; British and French financial competition in Turkey; etc.), her deteriorating military situation (Russian railway construction and an enormous army increase, the introduction of three years' military service in France) and, above all, the political cul-de-sac confronting the ruling elites on the home front (symbolized by the Reichstag elections of January 1912, when the dreaded socialists not only emerged as the largest party in the Reichstag, with one third of the popular vote, but demonstrated that they could, after all, co-operate successfully with liberal and left-liberal forces at the national level), popular and government imperialists began to accept the topos of inevitable war.[6] Business men were heard to utter the slogan, 'Better an end to terror than terror without end', and Moltke, the Chief of the General Staff, greeted the prospect of war with his famous comment: 'the sooner, the better'. Even Bethmann Hollweg, according to Fischer, was ready for war *(kriegswillig)*, eager for war *(kriegslustig)* and actively wanted a great war *(den grossen Krieg herbeigewünscht)*.[7] Well before July 1914, both popular and official imperialists had come to accept the possibility of war as a means, perhaps the only remaining means, of extricating the nation from the crisis situation into which it had got itself by dint of its headlong pursuit of 'world empire'.

The ruling classes' response to the perceived crisis was to organize the 'Leipzig cartel' of August 1913, when the Junkers and their big-business allies attempted to rally all patriotic forces, lower middle-class elements included, to a programme of vigorously anti-democratic and anti-socialist repression at home and an aggressively expansionist external policy that would not shrink from war. This required that certain pre-conditions be met (the Social Democrats had to be got on side, Russia must be cast in the role of aggressor, British neutrality must be secured), and the preparations actually undertaken included two new German army increases, a press campaign against the 'Russian peril' to arouse the people psychologically, diplomatic initiatives to win and consolidate alliances (including further neutrality overtures to Britain) and the creation of a war-planning body to make the necessary financial and economic arrangements. The kind of war envisaged was a short war of European rather than global dimensions, i.e., a war against France and Russia (all other military contingency plans were now lapsed) for mastery of the European Continent. It was, so Fischer stressed, an aggressive war of imperial expansion in the grand manner; it was not a preventive war born of 'fear and desperation'.

In this view the July crisis of 1914 was relatively unimportant, for German policy then, as previously, was really determined by such fundamental forces as the intensity of German nationalism and the pipe-dreams of Wilhelmine opinion-makers. From the very beginning of the crisis, so Fischer argued, the attitude of the German government was summed up in the 'now or never' slogan coined by the Kaiser.[8] In the first week of the crisis Germany gave Austria-Hungary the famous 'blank cheque' to crush Serbia, believing that this would almost certainly result in a European war. When Austrian delays and Russian reasonableness began to unmask German policy and to alert Britain in particular, the German leaders still made no sincere effort to restrain the Austrians even after it became apparent that British neutrality was a chimera. Thus the aggressive character of German imperialism, and the concomitant policy of the German political leaders, constituted the one factor that made a great war a certainty in August 1914. To this extent, Germany was, in Fischer's view, more responsible than other powers for the outbreak of the First World War.

The ensuing debate between Fischer and his critics has been chronicled by John Moses and others.[9] By the early 1980s a situation had been reached where the revisionist position of Fay, Barnes and others had been emphatically rejected in favour of the view that 'German policy in 1914 was dictated by considerations of a preventative war and bore a major responsibility for the chain of events which brought about the First World War'.[10] At last it was widely acknowledged that Fischer had 'thrown out a challenge both in his approach and in his conclusions' and that 'irrespective of whether one shares these conclusions, no-one will look at the origins of the First World War again in the same light as they were before 1961'.[11] It seemed clear that, whatever else they had achieved, Fischer and his school had finally laid to rest the legend tht in 1914 all the Great Powers had, in Lloyd George's now hackneyed phrase, 'slithered over the brink into the boiling cauldron of war', and that the Imperial government and the German power elites of big business and Junkerdom were therefore entirely innocent of responsibility for the outbreak of the First World War.[12]

Just when the arguments over German war aims and the character of Wilhelmine imperialism appeared to have abated once and for all, Fischer became embroiled in a fresh controversy. At its centre was Professor Karl Dietrich Erdmann of Kiel, a conservative historian, editor of the influential journal *Geschichte in Wissenschaft und Unterricht (GWU)* and a sometime holder of many of the highest offices in the West German and international historical profession. Over two decades Erdmann had been one of Fischer's most trenchant and consistent critics, travelling far and wide to spread the gospel of Fischer's alleged unreliability and aberrant *Verbohrtheit* (pig-headedness). Erdmann's chief evidentiary base, and the principal weapon in the arsenal of most of Fischer's opponents, had long been the diary of Kurt Riezler (private secretary and confidant of the last peacetime Imperial Chancellor, Theobald von Bethmann Hollweg), which Erdmann finally published, edited and introduced by himself, in 1972.[13] To the lucky handful who had been permitted to see the diaries in manuscript form – Fischer was not among them – and in the estimation of many who read Erdmann's published edition, Riezler's testimony appeared to corroborate the view that in 1914 Germany had neither wanted nor initiated a European war but merely, and at worst, run the risk of such a conflagration.[14] At this point – in 1983 – two publications appeared, apparently quite coincidentally. One was a polemic by Fischer (directed, in the main, at such old enemies as Erdmann, Egmont Zechlin and Andreas Hillgruber) entitled *July 1914: We Did not Slither Into It. The State Secret of the Riezler Diaries: A Polemic.* The other was an essay in the prestigious *Historische Zeitschrift* in which a young German historian named Bernd Sösemann re-examined the Erdmann edition of the Riezler diaries in respect of their genuineness, originality and authenticity.[15] By casting serious doubt on the value of the Riezler diaries as admissible historical evidence and, in particular, by questioning the authenticity of eight entries (from 7 July 1914 to 27 July 1914, and that of August 1914), and by demonstrating fairly conclusively that the diaries were quite unserviceable as proof that the Imperial German government was innocent of responsibility for the outbreak of the First World War, these publications together provided the inherently inflammable war-origins debate with a brief Indian summer in the form of a 'Riezler diaries controversy'. Beyond this, however, the Riezler diaries controversy yielded very little, and most scholars would probably share Wolfgang Mommsen's cautious estimate of its significance as 'the latest, and most likely the last stage in a long generational struggle about the painful political and ideological reorientation of German historical scholarship after the collapse of the Third Reich'.[16]

In a sense, the present work represents the culmination of Fischer's life's work. In 1961 he introduced his first book by expressing the hope that it would offer the reader 'pointers to fields wider than its own, for it indicates certain mental attitudes and aspirations which were active in German policy during the First World War and remained operative later. Seen from this angle, it may serve as a contribution towards the problem of the continuity of German policy from the First World War to the Second.' He concluded this study with the observation that:

> Germany overtaxed herself in the First World War as the result of an obstinate underestimate of the strength of others and over-estimate of her own. This permanent misconception of realities forms a 'continuity of error' which goes back far into the world policy of the reign of Wilhelm II ... But even after the defeat of 1918, many Germans, and especially those who had played leading parts in political and economic life up to 1918, preserved in the two following decades a political and historical image of themselves which was coloured by illusions.[17]

During the 1960s and 1970s Fischer was to allude to this theme again and again, and it was possibly this assertion of lines of continuity from Imperial Germany to Hitler's Germany which most rankled with his German critics and least impressed his well-wishers at home and abroad. Thus, quite recently, Alan Milward, for some strange reason, expressed the bizarre view that 'speculation about ... the supposed peculiarities of German political thought and tradition is escapism'.[18] Other critics have imputed to Fischer a kind of inverted nationalism, operating on the assumption that 'if we Germans can't be the best, we must be worst'. Nevertheless, the present work offers the most detailed statement of Fischer's continuity thesis to date. It may therefore be read as a summing-up of the work of the Fischer School, but it is important, too, as a lead-in to the related but not synonymous *Sonderweg* debate (over the alleged uniqueness of the German path to modernity).

There are three main approaches that Fischer might have adopted in his endeavour to explain the alleged continuity in modern German history. He might have followed Ludwig Dehio and opted for a geographical and geopolitical approach.[19] Alternatively, he might have focused primarily on German militarism and the German mind, on the survival, in other words, of pre-industrial ideas and political mentalities. There were many cogent reasons why he should adopt such an approach, including the examples of Herbert Spencer and Josef Schumpeter, to say nothing of the compelling force of the German tradition of philosophical idealism in which Fischer, no less than Gerhard Ritter or Egmont Zechlin, had been nurtured. Finally, Fischer might have taken a leaf out of Thorstein Veblen's *Imperial Germany and the Industrial Revolution* (1915) and highlighted the discrepancy between German economic development and Germany's relatively backward social values and political norms.[20] Although he attempted, to some degree at least, to accommodate all three explanatory models, Fischer has, at bottom, plumped rather heavily for the idealist approach. In essence, he argues that the basic continuity in German history between 1871 and 1945 was provided by the agrarian–big business alliance, which changed in form but not in regard to its substantive goals (the defence of power and privilege against liberalism and socialism), and that in crisis situations these elites resorted to domestic repression and external aggression.

Once again, Fischer found himself in deep water, particularly within Germany. Part of the difficulty may well be as trivial as literary style, for Fischer seeks to avoid what Gordon Craig has termed 'the deleterious effects of professorial profundity' by eschewing sociological jargon and other widely cherished forms of academic obscurantism.[21] But more serious criticisms have not been wanting. For example, it has been argued, in Germany and abroad, that Fischer's allegedly vague talk of 'pre-industrial' attitudes would be profitably replaced by more precise and comprehensive analysis of the German elites and by a more finely grained picture of the traditional political system and its dynamics. What we need here, according to K. H. Jarausch, is 'a broader rethinking of the relationship between bureaucratization, industrialization, national unification, and political participation'.[22] But is Fischer necessarily mistaken? He is certainly not alone in arguing as he does. Thus Fritz Ringer, for example:

As vehicles of a kind of cultural lag, European secondary schools and universities . . . contributed to one of the most fascinating and difficult problems in modern European social and cultural history: the survival of preindustrial social roles and attitudes into the industrial era. The point is not only that European aristocracies retained much influence and prestige until the twentieth century. Large segments of the middle class also refused to identify fully with the new world of industry and commerce.[23]

Echoing nineteenth-century British Radicals, Martin Wiener has demonstrated that even in Britain, where industrialization proceeded sedately, under almost ideal conditions, it was the landed gentry who finally managed to impose *their* view of the world on the captains of industry rather than vice versa, while Arno Mayer also argues persuasively that Europe's *anciens régimes*, which were 'thoroughly preindustrial and pre-bourgeois', were not finally set aside until defeated in 'the Thirty Years' War of the general crisis of the twentieth century'.[24]

Another extremely popular criticism has been the now familiar charge that Fischer was reading his history backwards: instead of contemplating Imperial Germany on its own terms, he saw it as a mere prelude to 1933. A third frequently encountered line of attack was the claim that Fischer's work was insufficiently grounded in systematic comparative research.[25]

Of course, the rush to the anti-Fischer colours on this issue may well represent, for foreign scholars at least, little more than a long overdue reversal of historiographical fashion, for the continuity thesis has such a long pedigree outside Germany as to have almost acquired the status of a self-evident truth, virtually compelling the historian to see 'all past as prologue – to Hitler'.[26] It is also worth recalling that not even Blackbourn and Eley deny the existence and importance of continuities in modern German history; they claim merely that 'the question about continuity is not *whether*, but *what kind?*'[27] It is certainly true that among the many who have sided with Fischer there has been a surfeit of vague generalization and hyperbole. Even Gordon Craig refers to 'the conservative-militaristic concern that had dominated politics in the Wilhelmine period, done everything possible to shorten the life of the Weimar Republic, and elevated him [Hitler] to power in 1933'.[28] But was it the same Old Gang, and why did they have to call in Hitler at all? Some commentators have attempted to specify what they understand by political culture, but can one then go on to trace a meaningful line of continuity from the political culture of Bismarck's Reich to that of the Federal Republic in the 1980s?[29] Is it legitimate to discern the cloven hoof of traditional illiberal nationalism in the neutralism of the present-day 'Green movement'? These are questions which can reasonably be asked and are being asked of supporters of the continuity thesis.[30]

How well Fischer has performed his task in relation to the continuity question is, of course, a matter which Germanless readers can now determine for themselves. Recent surveys of the voluminous literature have done little to dissolve the clouds of ambivalence and ambiguity. Thus Pierre Ayçoberry, in 1979: 'one cannot say for certain whether the Third Reich was a radical departure from or a continuation of the preceding regimes.' By 1983 Hiden and Farquharson seemed less unsure but nevertheless took an each-way bet by concluding: 'Hitler's bid for world power can no longer itself be seen as constituting the break with Germany's past. At the same time there was nothing in that past to prepare it for Auschwitz'. In 1985 Ian Kershaw said much the same, although he emphasized that 'few historians would now deny that Nazism arose from – and indeed temporarily bound together – a number of pronounced structural continuities in German society and politics linking Bismarck's and the Kaiser's Reich with Hitler's.'[31] Thanks to Fischer, some of these continuities are now perhaps more readily identifiable.[32]

Fischer's second major contribution to the writing of German history has been of a methodological nature – the reforming and modernizing impulse which he provided during the 1960s. Prior to the appearance of his *Griff nach der Weltmacht* in 1961, historical research in Germany – excluding East Germany or the GDR – had been dominated by the statist, conservative, nationalist, idealist and Rankean historicist model:

Well into the mid-twentieth century, German historians followed the model set by Leopold von Ranke of a narrative, event-oriented history which concentrated on politics narrowly conceived as the actions of government in pursuit of national interest *(raison d'état)* relatively unaffected by social and economic considerations. Moreover, since the mid-nineteenth century, German university-based histo-

rians have been committed to an interpretation of the
national past that saw the culmination of German history in
Bismarck's establishment of a German Empire under Prussian dominance, a state that maintained the privileged political position of the propertied classes and left considerable
authority in a monarchy surrounded by an aristocratic aura.
The methodological and political conservatism that characterized the German historical profession reflected the
'anachronistic' character of German political conditions, the
failure of parliamentary and democratic reform in a country
that had rapidly undergone economic modernization and
contained an industrial working class increasing in size and
political awareness . . . German historians . . . and
philosophers . . . asserted the 'idiographic' character of historical method concerned with 'understanding' *(Verstehen)*
unique human intentions and actions and the inapplicability
of methods seeking 'to explain' historical behavior
'nomologically' by means of abstractions or generalizations.
Neither 1918, 1933, nor 1945 initiated a profound reorientation in historiographical outlook.[33]

Impervious to foreign stimuli, this remarkably robust tradition
outlived all domestic challenges – from Karl Lamprecht through
to Eckart Kehr and Hans Rosenberg[34] – and survived the most
drastic metamorphoses in the wider socio-political environment
(the First World War and the revolution of 1918, the Weimar
democracy and the Great Depression, the Third Reich and the
collapse of 1945) only to succumb at last, in the 1960s, to the
challenge presented by Fischer and his school.

Why Fischer, when so many others had made so little impression? In 1931 Gerhard Ritter described Eckart Kehr as a 'pure-
bred Bolshevik' who 'should habilitate – now, if possible – in
Russia, where he naturally belongs'. In the face of such intoler-
ance, Kehr was forced to emigrate, not to the Soviet Union, but
to the United States, where he died in 1933. Wehler records a
very different response to the Fischer heresy, which was, of
course, no less roundly and maliciously condemned by the conservative establishment within the German historical *Zunft*
(guild), but applauded yet more vigorously by the younger gen-

eration of historians, in open and successful defiance of the 'gerarchi':

> In 1961 a noted German historian with whom I had hoped to discuss Fischer's first book responded to my query in the following way: 'It is absolutely incomprehensible to me how a German historian not living in Leipzig could write such a pamphlet.' An icy silence met my suggestion that it was indeed fortunate that the author in fact did not live in the GDR but in Hamburg and so could even be invited to participate in a discussion.[35]

Fischer was neither driven into exile nor silenced; in time, he prevailed against his adversaries to the point of being hailed by 1975 as the champion of a 'new orthodoxy'.[36]

An important reason why Fischer succeeded where others had failed was the uniquely hospitable environment in which Fischer threw down the gauntlet to the German historical establishment. By the early 1960s a new 'democratic' generation was emerging which rightly felt that National Socialism, the Second World War and the collapse of 1945 had discredited the old paradigm,[37] its credibility being further eroded by the impact of returning emigrants, the new opportunities for study abroad (especially in the USA) and the innovative initiatives of a few centres of excellence within Germany itself – for example, the Free University of Berlin, Tübingen, Heidelberg (Werner Conze) and Cologne (Theodor Schieder). The economic prosperity provided by the 'economic miracle', the thaw in the Cold War and the end of conservative government in Germany (1966/69) resulted in unprecedented university expansion and reform: the number of universities doubled, new chairs were created and university administration was reformed and democratized. The German historical profession received an infusion of new blood that was not possible before or since, and the prevailing social climate shifted from complacent and conformist consumerism to a new spirit of bold and optimistic liberal reformism. West German historians began to ask new questions of the past and to seek answers by exploring uncharted terrain. The Fischer controversy was thus more or less coeval with other debates – on the German revolution of 1918 and the workers councils movement, on National Socialism, on social and economic history, on the 'primacy of domestic politics' and the German *Sonderweg* (separate path to modernity), as well as on a variety of theoretical issues. That Fischer was not alone ensured that he would not be ignored.

What made him all the more untouchable, if not entirely acceptable to the German academic establishment, was the fact that he was not, as Kehr had been, a radical outsider.[38] On the contrary, he made his journey to Damascus at a time when he had already been for many years an *Ordinarius* (full professor and head of department) at the University of Hamburg. There was no possibility that his work could be 'killed by silence' *(totgeschwiegen)*. The pill may have been sweetened somewhat by the fact that Fischer's methodology was not, after all, so unreservedly revolutionary. To the extent that he and his colleagues still focused primarily on elites and high politics, remained very much in the familiar idealist mould and continued to present an analysis that was traditionalist in its emphasis on, or at least in its failure to ignore, narration and personalities, they were persons with whom the defenders of the old paradigm felt able to enter into dialogue. As yet, there was still no real social history as such, and the Fischerites made only limited, *ad hoc* forays into the field of economic history.[39]

Intelligible or not, the threat posed by Fischer was a serious one. To begin with, he managed 'to stand on its head a conservative historiographical tradition which glorified the *Sonderweg*'. Once a positive virtue (at least in conservative eyes), the peculiarities of the Germans were now endowed with new meaning and identified as the source of many of Germany's woes in the twentieth century.[40] A second notable innovation (or inversion) was Fischer's advocacy of the 'primacy of domestic politics' (the notion that the sources of Imperial Germany's conduct in the international arena must be sought in her domestic political, economic and social ideas and institutions) in place of the hitherto sacrosanct doctrine of 'the primacy of foreign policy', which asserted that only war, diplomacy and high politics really mattered, and that such questions were normally decided by a handful of political actors motivated by *raison d'état* and acting with little or no reference to internal social, economic or political pressures. It may be doubted whether 'Fischer learned much from Eckart Kehr',[41] but it can no longer be doubted that after Fischer the study of German foreign relations in the modern era was radically different from everything that had gone before. The domestic politics of the *Kaiserreich* (Imperial Germany) were now also examined on a broad front, closer attention being paid to economic interests, social structures, public opinion and political culture than ever before. In a very real sense, it is true to say that 'in the long run Fischer's methodological emphasis on the need to focus on the interaction of Imperial domestic and foreign policy . . . has been at least as influential as his substantive conclusion that the German government was primarily responsible for the First World War'.[42]

This methodological challenge had a number of important consequences. Most obviously perhaps, the Fischer initiative inspired, directly or indirectly, a plethora of important new studies of modern German history, particularly in relation to the *Kaiserreich*. Wilhelmine imperialism, conceived of as the product of a dynamic interaction between domestic and foreign determinants, was put under the microscope as never before, while an imposing body of meticulously thorough research was undertaken into the institutional, socio-economic and ideological factors which conditioned German policy and on the roles of particular crises and individuals.[43] At the same time, Fischer and his colleagues effectively discredited the historicist paradigm and opened up the German historical profession to the bracing winds of international competition and co-operation.

Although Fischer retired in 1973, the 'revolution' in German historiography continued to gather momentum, the rebel headquarters moving south to the new University of Bielefeld, where two young professors of modern history, Hans-Ulrich Wehler and Jürgen Kocka, extended and broadened the work of the Hamburg School, taking into their ranks many former 'Fischerites' and functioning as a beacon and an inspiration to many of the best and brightest among the nation's younger historians. This new generation of West German historians has been variously styled – for example, 'Kehrites' (a highly misleading and no longer popular tag), structural-functionalists (referring to the dominant methodology),[44] critico-historical social scientists (as they see themselves) and Bielefelders (as I, and others, have called them, perhaps imperfectly, but for want of a more precise label). What they popularized during the 1970s, and continue to practise in the 1980s, is an eclectic and distinctively German social history of politics.[45]

Influenced primarily by Max Weber and Otto Hintze but also, via the Frankfurt School, by Karl Marx, and to a considerable extent as well by US social-science methods, the Bielefelders insisted that while there could be no satisfactory general theory of history, the writing of history must be theoretically informed and that the necessary theoretical infrastructures could be borrowed on an *ad hoc* basis from the social sciences. They further insisted that the historian must approach the past with a critical perspective (in practice, this usually meant a left-liberal or Social Democratic as well as a comparative perspective), that the work of the historian should possess contemporary relevance and serve a present emancipatory function, and, above all, that it be societal history *(Gesellschaftsgeschichte)* – in others words, that the historian pay less attention to personalities, particularities or narrative and concentrate rather on producing structural history offering political, economic and cultural syntheses. The Bielefelders are most heavily indebted, though not uncritically so, to modernization theory,[46] and the theoretical constructs which have characterized their work include the concept of organized capitalism, that of *Sammlungspolitik* (consensus politics), the theory of the primacy of domestic politics, the Bonapartism model, the theory of social imperialism and the *Sonderweg* thesis.[47] The *loci classici* of the Bielefeld school are Wehler's *Das Deutsche Kaiserreich 1871–1918* (1973) and Kocka's *Klassengesellschaft im Krieg* (1973).[48]

Evidently better organized than the Fischer school, the Bielefelders' entrepreneurial skills found outlets in new journals and publishing ventures. Their *Geschichte und Gesellschaft: Zeitschrift für Historische Sozialwissenschaft (History and Society: Journal of Historical Social Science)*, though launched only in 1975, now enjoys a professional standing which is probably equal to, if it has not surpassed, that of the venerable *Historische Zeitschrift*. Also well established by now is the pedagogic journal *Geschichtsdidaktik* (1976). Individual Bielefelders have been astonishingly prolific, and their various publication series have proved to be uniformly successful and widely respected. Their *Critical Studies* series *(Kritische Studien zur Geschichtswissenschaft)*, for example, has alone produced well over sixty major volumes by the mid-1980s. Such productivity, combined with their tolerance of opposition and criticism, their openness to innovative impulses from abroad, their willingness to employ comparative methods and to participate in international projects, no less than their vaguely anti-establishment radicalism, won the Bielefelders a wide following among the then younger generation (now middle generation) of German historians. Although they and their admirers in reality never amounted to much more than a conspicuously colourful minority within the West German historical profession as a whole, the Bielefelders were undoubtedly the most widely remarked and the most innovative force at work in German historical studies during the decade of the 1970s.[49]

By the early 1980s the postwar revolution in German historiography was beginning to devour its own children. Yet another generation was emerging, in whose eyes Fischer was ancient history and the Bielefelders belonged in medieval mothballs. Responding partly to the promptings of the Bielefelders themselves,[50] younger historians began experimenting with history written 'from below', 'from within' and 'from the periphery'. Subjects deemed worthy of investigation, often for the very first time, included the peasantry, the urban working class, local history, proto-industrialization, piety, death, insanity, sexual behaviour, women, the family and everyday life under National Socialism. Methods employed by the new 'grassroots social historians' ranged from oral history and quantification to historical demography and historical anthropology. To date, only psycho-history appears to have made little impact.[51] While the majority of practitioners of this 'new social history' in the Federal Republic have gone about their business of recovering the everyday experience of the past with minimal or no reference to the critico-historical social science of Bielefeld – most manifest greater interest in the work of the French *Annales* school and seem to be more impressed by studies like E. P. Thompson's *The*

Making of the English Working Class (1963) or Rhys Isaac's Pulitzer Prize-winning *The Transformation of Virginia 1740–1790* (1982) than by Wehler's *Bismarck und der Imperialismus* (1969) – two strands of the German 'new social history' have been obviously and deliberately critical of the work pioneered by Fischer and developed by Wehler, Kocka and their school. These are, on the one hand, a small and disparate band of neo-Marxists, many of their best practitioners being British or American and devotees of currently popular heterodoxies, such as those of Antonio Gramsci and Nicos Poulantzas.[52] One of their number recently summed up their case against the work of Fischer and the Bielefelders as follows:

> First, it portrays too static a picture of German history and does not sufficiently allow for social and political change. Secondly, it ascribes too much to the manipulative wizardry of the political elites and neglects the independent effect on the political system of the allegedly manipulated groups in German society. Thirdly, it exaggerates the extent to which the ruling groups in late nineteenth- and early twentieth-century German society were 'feudal' or 'pre-industrial' or 'traditional' in their outlook at a time when Germany was already a highly industrialized capitalist economy.[53]

On the other hand, there is also a growing number of increasingly voluble grassroots historians of everyday life practising, in the main, unconventional methods whose work is either deliberately or implicitly anti-Bielefeld.[54] Beginning in November 1982, efforts have been made to organize these diverse groups (academics and non-academics, professionals and amateur enthusiasts, Marxists and non-Marxists) into a nationwide History Workshop *(Geschichtswerkstatt)* which has already held several meetings and festivals and come to be linked, by friend and foe alike, with the political 'Green' movement.[55]

Where all this will lead is uncertain. Clearly, historical studies in West Germany today exhibit greater methodological, theoretical and ideological pluralism than ever before, and the present situation is one of great fluidity. It may be that the pendulum has swung so far in the direction of diversity that the profession now confronts the threat of fragmentation.[56] To most observers, however, present circumstances offer greater cause for satisfaction and congratulation than for anxiety. Either way, we are indebted to Fritz Fischer. While it would be misleading to attribute all the exciting developments of the last quarter-century to the Fischer initiative of the early 1960s, it would certainly be fallacious and churlish not to recognize that few of the innovations that have occurred, from Wehler through to Alf Lüdtke[57] and the German history workshop movement, would have been possible in Germany if Fischer had not ventured to heed Thucydides' dictum that 'one cannot rely on every detail that has come down to us by way of tradition'. When he chose to re-examine Germany's part in the 'thirty years' war' of 1914–45,[58] Fischer began a revolution in German historiography. It may be debated whether he provided a necessary or a sufficient cause, but what is now established beyond reasonable doubt is that 'the first impulse drawing widespread attention to social history there [in Germany] was the campaign by the Fischer School to demonstrate the "primacy of domestic politics" in foreign policy decisions . . . The Germans' view of social history has been molded in large measure by the numerous monographs . . . published by students and admirers of Fischer.'[59]

There is a further dimension to Fischer's reformist or revolutionary activities. As an eminent American historian recently remarked, many of the methodological disputes among post-1945 German historians, and even quarrels over substantive issues like the continuity question and the 'German way', have really 'derived ultimately not from differences regarding scholarly research but from differences regarding the moral and didactic function of history'.[60] To take an obvious example, West German historians have always been under considerable pressure from their East German colleagues, who insisted from the very beginning that they alone had made a clean break with the past, whereas the Federal Republic was merely the successor state to Hitler's Reich.[61] But even in Imperial Germany, 'the German problem had an academic dimension'.[62] Believing that 'it is by facing the obscure forces within us and the unpleasant truths about ourselves that nations, like individuals, can cope with the world around them and face the future',[63] Fischer set out to persuade his compatriots that 'fault lay not with Hitler but with the Germans who followed him'.[64]

It was perfectly natural that an *Ordinarius* born in 1908 should see himself in this light. From the late nineteenth century onwards, German professors, and German historians in particular, had enjoyed enormous public esteem as 'bearers of culture', as 'the closest thing to a "priestly caste" that German society has known', as 'prophets to their people' and arbiters of public opinion.[65] As recently as the 1950s and 1960s 'opinion polls . . . regularly showed them as being more admired than bishops, ministers of state, general directors of business concerns, military commanders and other dignitaries'.[66] Traditionally, a professor of history, as Fischer was in the late fifties and sixties, was in a position to exert a powerful influence in public life. Unlike most of his peers, Fischer chose not to put his influence at the disposal of a restored 'old regime' but rather, as his preface to this book makes clear, to participate in the cause of educating his compatriots for democracy and maturity.[67]

It is too soon to say whether he has had any significant and lasting success in this field. Many of the cognoscenti are pessimistic. It is often alleged, for example, that the past two or three decades have witnessed a dramatic decline in historical consciousness in West Germany, particularly among the young, who regard the past as being largely irrelevant.[68] We are also frequently told that the same period has seen a steady erosion of professorial status in the Federal Republic, due to the loss of status incurred through the popular perception of the universities as purveyors of obsolete values and their connivance at the triumph of National Socialism in 1933, due also to the supplanting of the old education-based status hierarchy by a modern class hierarchy, and to the apparent lowering of standards consequent on the alleged failure of the education reform movement of the 1960s and 1970s.[69] Thus Professor Hans Mommsen sees it as being highly significant that during the Hitler Diaries fiasco foreign experts were the first to be consulted.[70] Volker Berghahn is still more pessimistic, doubting whether Fischer has won the day even in respect of his substantive points.[71]

Yet there are also grounds for optimism. German democracy is now firmly established on a sure foundation of massive popular support, and the old values are fast giving way to new ones, if they have not disappeared altogether. Bonn is not Weimar, so the saying goes, and there is now a mass audience for the Fischers and the Wehlers. In fact, the outsiders of yesteryear are now part – albeit only a part – of the current intellectual establishment, and technological progress has given them opportunities never before available to such gadflies:

> Their direct political influence has always been small despite the fact that there are now many more of them than in the past . . . Indirectly, through television, newspapers, periodicals and publishing houses and, generally speaking, as disseminators of ideas, as the makers of public opinion, their influence has been out of proportion to their numbers. This is also true with regard to their role in education.[72]

Until very recently the pundits were all agreed that the Germans were no longer a people with a sense of history and that the historical profession in Germany was very much a debased coinage. Recent developments seem to have disproven this claim. There have been, of late, numerous historical festivals and exhibitions, such as the Berlin Prussian exhibition which opened in August 1981, and these have turned out, rather unexpectedly, to be immensely popular and successful. The new grassroots or 'barefoot' social history movement affords ample testimony to the fact that ordinary men and women in the Federal Republic *are* greatly interested in their past, but in the *whole* past, including that of the 'little man' and other historical losers. These enthusiastic amateurs may be, as their critics maintain, more than a little naïve and romantic, but they do not shy away from awkward questions about the past, as did their parents and grandparents, and there are no more historical taboos in Germany today – except, of course, in the 'workers' and peasants' state' to the east. Fischer and like-minded colleagues have striven to make a positive contribution to such salutary developments. If, as Walter Laqueur asserts, 'there is now not only more freedom in Germany than ever before in her history, but also more common sense and moderation',[73] Fischer must surely be credited with having had a hand in this. If so, he merits recognition as an historian of rare distinction, for 'there are not many historians . . . whose works have changed the way people see themselves.'[74]

In the end, two things can be said of Fischer with a large degree of certainty. Firstly, his work on the First World War – on German war aims and on the origins of the conflict – has become almost as widely accepted and as closely associated with his explicandum as is Thucydides' work on the Great Peloponnesian War of antiquity. In respect of Fischer and the First World War of 1914–18, one would be fully justified in applying to Fischer H. T. Wade-Gery's judgement of Thucydides: 'readers of all opinions will probably agree that he saw more truly, inquired more responsibly, and reported more faithfully than any other [contemporary] historian.'[75] Secondly, the Fischer impulse has proved to be exceptionally fruitful, methodologically as well as empirically, both at home and internationally. In the age of nuclear war and 'mutual assured destruction', international relations experts still feel that they may safely draw on the 'lessons of 1914' as interpreted by Fischer and his school.[76] But has Fischer really helped to change the Germans? He tried. Only time will tell how well he, and those who tried with him, actually succeeded.

Roger Fletcher

Notes: Introduction

1 Guenther Roth, 'Review essay: Comparative evidence and historical judgment', *American Journal of Sociology*, vol. 86, no. 6 (1981), p. 1422.
2 Keith Robbins, *The First World War* (Oxford, 1985), p. 166.
3 Fritz Fischer, *Germany's Aims in the First World War* (New York, 1967), pp. 607–8. This is the English translation of his *Griff nach der Weltmacht* (1961).
4 See Fritz Fischer, *World Power or Decline: The Controversy over Germany's Aims in the First World War*, trans. Lancelot L. Farrar, Robert Kimber and Rita Kimber (New York and London, 1974).
5 English translation, by Marian Jackson, entitled *War of Illusions: German Policies from 1911 to 1914* (London and New York, 1975).
6 On the extent to which even the socialists had fallen prey to the dominant ideology of aggressive nationalism, see Roger Fletcher, *Revisionism & Empire: Socialist Imperialism in Germany 1897–1914* (London, 1984). Other valuable English-language studies of Wilhelmine nationalism include Geoff Eley, *Reshaping the German Right: Radical Nationalism and Political Change after Bismarck* (New Haven, 1980); David Blackbourn, *Class, Religion, and Local Politics in Wilhelmine Germany: The Center Party in Württemberg before 1914* (New Haven, 1980); and Roger Chickering, *We Men Who Feel Most German: A Cultural Study of the Pan-German League, 1886–1914* (London, 1984).
7 Fritz Fischer, *Juli 1914: Wir sind nicht hineingeschlittert. Das Staatsgeheimnis um die Riezler-Tagebücher: Eine Streitschrift* (Reinbek bei Hamburg, 1983), p. 113.
8 On 3 or 4 July the Kaiser sided with the General Staff and annotated Ambassador Tschirschky's despatch from Vienna (of 30 June 1914) 'now or never' and to the effect that 'the Serbs must be disposed of, *and* that right *soon!*' Tschirschky, Zimmermann and the political and diplomatic leadership in general then at once fell into line behind this apparent 'order' from the 'All-Highest'. See Imanuel Geiss (ed.), *July 1914. The Outbreak of the First World War: Selected Documents* (London, 1967), pp. 62, 64–5.
9 See John A. Moses, *The War Aims of Imperial Germany: Professor Fritz Fischer and His Critics* (St Lucia, 1968); idem, *The Politics of Illusion: The Fischer Controversy in German Historiography* (London, 1975); Wolfgang Jäger, *Historische Forschung und politische Kultur in Deutschland: Die Debatte 1914–1980 über den Ausbruch des Ersten Weltkrieges* (Göttingen, 1984), pp. 132–57.
10 W. J. Mommsen, untitled review article in the Bulletin of the German Historical Institute in London, no. 14 (autumn 1983), p. 28 (hereafter cited as GHIL Bulletin).

11 H. W. Koch, 'Introduction', in Koch (ed.), *The Origins of the First World War*, 2nd edn (London, 1984), p. 25. This tribute from an avowed opponent of Fischer is high praise indeed. Other critics have agreed that Fischer was 'entirely correct' in arguing that 'the war Bethmann unleashed was indeed a grasp at world power' (David E. Kaiser, 'Germany and the origins of the First World War', *Journal of Modern History*, vol. 55, no. 3 (1983), p. 468). Even among American international relations experts, often disdainful of 'antiquarian historiography', one now finds complete acceptance. Thus Stephen Van Evera: 'I am satisfied that the "Fischer School" have proven their argument that German prewar intentions were very aggressive' ('Why Cooperation Failed in 1914', *World Politics*, vol. 38, no. 1 (1985), p. 100 n. 70).

12 David Lloyd George, *War Memoirs*, Vol. 1 (London, 1933), p. 52. On the German 'innocence campaign', see Ulrich Heinemann, *Die verdrängte Niederlage: Politische Öffentlichkeit und Kriegsschuldfrage in der Weimarer Republik* (Göttingen, 1983), and Jäger, *Historische Forschung*, pp. 44–117.

13 Kurt Riezler, *Tagebücher, Aufsätze, Dokumente*, ed. Karl Dietrich Erdmann (Göttingen, 1972).

14 Fritz Stern, 'Bethmann Hollweg and the War: The Bounds of Responsibility', in Stern, *The Failure of Illiberalism: Essays on the Political Culture of Modern Germany*, Phoenix edn (Chicago and London, 1975) (first published 1967), pp. 77–118; Konrad H. Jarausch, 'The illusion of limited war: Chancellor Bethmann Hollweg's calculated risk, July 1914', *Central European History*, vol. 2, no. 1 (1969), pp. 48–76; idem, *The Enigmatic Chancellor: Bethmann Hollweg and the Hubris of Imperial Germany* (New Haven and London, 1972); Kaiser, 'Germany and the origins of the First World War', pp. 442–74.

15 Fischer, *Juli 1914*; Bernd Sösemann, 'Die Tagebücher Kurt Riezlers: Untersuchungen zu ihrer Echtheit und Edition', *Historische Zeitschrift*, vol. 236. (1983), pp. 327–69. Similar criticism had been expressed a decade previously, in two reviews of the Riezler Diaries – by Fritz Fellner in *Mitteilungen der Österreichischen Geschichtsforschung*, Vol. 81 (1973), pp. 490–95, and Bernd Sösemann in *Blätter für deutsche Landesgeschichte*, Vol. 110 (1974), pp. 261–75.

16 GHIL Bulletin, p. 33.

17 Fischer, *Germany's Aims*, pp. xxii, 636–7.

18 Alan S. Milward, 'It can happen here', *London Review of Books*, vol. 7, no. 8 (2.5.1985), p. 5. As a corrective, see David Blackbourn and Geoff Eley, *The Peculiarities of German History: Bourgeois Society and Politics in Nineteenth-Century Germany* (Oxford, 1984), pp. 28–31. There is certainly no shortage of evidence from contemporary observers testifying to the peculiarities of the Germans. See, for example, *Behind the Lines. One Woman's War: The Letters of Caroline Ethel Cooper*, ed. Decie Denholm (London, 1982), pp. 84–5, 120, 129, 194.

19 For a recent application of this type of approach, see David Calleo, *The*

German Problem Reconsidered (Cambridge, 1978). For a trenchant critique of the book and its method, see Hans-Ulrich Wehler, *Preussen ist wieder chic: Politik und Polemik* (Frankfurt, 1983), pp. 60–7.

20 See Harold James, 'The Problem of Continuity in German History: The Interwar Years', *Historical Journal*, vol. 27, no. 2 (1984), pp. 513–14; Blackbourn and Eley, *Peculiarities*, pp. 5–6. Veblen has recently been described as 'the first scholar, in Europe as well as America, to play down the role of Otto von Bismarck and to approach modern German history from what today would be called a "structuralist" point of view' (John P. Diggins, *The Bard of Savagery: Thorstein Veblen and Modern Social Theory* (New York, 1978), p. 200).

21 G. A. Craig, *The Germans* (New York, 1982), p. 318.

22 Konrad H. Jarausch, 'German Social History – American Style', *Journal of Social History*, vol. 18, no. 2 (1985), p. 20 (all page numbers refer to an earlier draft version).

23 Fritz K. Ringer, *Education and Society in Modern Europe* (Bloomington, IN, 1979), p. 7. Konrad Jarausch feels this thesis is 'overstated' but he does not deny its general validity. Cf. K. H. Jarausch, *The Transformation of Higher Learning 1860–1930* (Chicago, 1983), p. 33.

24 Martin J. Wiener, *English Culture and the Decline of the Industrial Spirit 1850–1980* (Cambridge, 1981); Arno J. Mayer, *The Persistence of the Old Regime: Europe to the Great War* (London, 1981), pp. 3, 4 and *passim*.

25 See, for example, Thomas Nipperdey, '1933 und Kontinuität der deutschen Geschichte', *Historische Zeitschrift*, vol. 227 (1978), pp. 86–111; K. H. Jarausch, 'From Second to Third Reich: The problem of continuity in German foreign policy', *Central European History*, vol. 12, no. 1 (1979), pp. 68–82; Klaus Hildebrand, 'Staatskunst oder Systemzwang? Die "deutsche Frage" als Problem der Weltpolitik', *Historische Zeitschrift*, vol. 228 (1979), pp. 624–44; idem, *The Third Reich* (London, 1984), pp. 110–11, 159–63; idem, 'Julikrise 1914: Das europäische Sicherheitsdilemma', *GWU*, vol. 36, no. 7 (1985), pp. 469–502; Andreas Hillgruber, *Kontinuität und Diskontinuität in der deutschen Aussenpolitik von Bismarck bis Hitler* (Düsseldorf, 1969); idem, *Germany and the Two World Wars* (London, 1981); idem, *Endlich genug über Nationalsozialismus und Zweiten Weltkrieg? Forschungsstand und Literatur* (Düsseldorf, 1982), pp. 48–56; Geoff Eley, 'What produces fascism: Preindustrial conditions or a crisis of a capitalist state?' *Politics and Society*, vol. 12, no. 2 (1983), pp. 53–82; Richard J. Evans, 'The Myth of Germany's Missing Revolution', *The New Left Review*, no. 149 (1985), pp. 67–96.

26 Peter Gay, *Freud, Jews, and Other Germans: Masters and Victims in Modernist Culture* (Oxford, 1978), p. 7. Among the numerous historians who have endorsed the continuity thesis in one form or another are John C. G. Röhl (ed.), *From Bismarck to Hitler: The Problem of Continuity in German History* (London, 1970); Hermann Glaser, *The Cultural Roots of National Socialism* (London, 1978); H.-U. Wehler, *The German Empire 1871–1918* (Leamington Spa, 1985); E. J. Feuchtwanger (ed.), *Upheaval*

and Continuity: A Century of German History (London, 1973); Wilhelm Alff (ed.), *Materialien zum Kontinuitätsproblem der deutschen Geschichte* (Frankfurt, 1976); idem, *Deutschlands Sonderung von Europa 1862–1945* (Frankfurt, 1984); Bernd Faulenbach, *Ideologie des deutschen Weges: Die deutsche Geschichte in der Historiographie zwischen Kaiserreich und Nationalsozialismus* (Munich, 1980); idem, '"Deutscher Sonderweg": Zur Geschichte und Problematik einer zentralen Kategorie des deutschen geschichtlichen Bewusstseins', *Aus Politik und Zeitgeschichte*, B33/81 (15.8.1981), pp. 2–21; Peter Reichel, *Politische Kultur der Bundesrepublik* (Opladen, 1981); Hans Mommsen, 'Die deutschen Eliten und der Mythos des nationalen Aufbruchs von 1933', *Merkur*, vol. 38, no. 1 (1984), pp. 97–102; Hagen Schulze, 'Die Versuchung des Absoluten: Zur deutschen politischen Kultur im 19. und 20. Jahrhundert', *Aus Politik und Zeitgeschichte*, B7/84 (18.2.1984), pp. 3–10.

27 Blackbourn and Eley, *Peculiarities*, p. 22.
28 G. A. Craig, *Germany 1866–1945* (New York, 1980), p. 673.
29 See Reichel, *Politische Kultur*, pp. 105–6; Hans Mommsen, 'The burden of the past', in Jürgen Habermas (ed.), *Observations on 'The Spiritual Situation of the Age'*, trans. A. Buchwalter (Cambridge, Mass., 1984), p. 280; Craig, *The Germans*, pp. 10–11; Wehler, *The German Empire*, pp. 245–6.
30 See Wehler, 'Wir brauchen keinen neuen deutschen Sonderweg', *Frankfurter Allgemeine Zeitung*, no. 38 (15.2.1982), p. 9, and several similar contributions reprinted in Wehler, *Preussen ist wieder chic*. For useful discussions, see Dan Diner, 'The "National Question" in the Peace Movement: Origins and tendencies', *New German Critique*, no. 28 (1983), pp. 86–107; Hans Mommsen, 'History and national identity: The case of Germany', *German Studies Review*, vol. 6, no. 3 (1983), pp. 559–82.
31 Pierre Ayçoberry, *The Nazi Question: An Essay on the Interpretations of National Socialism (1922–1975)* (New York, 1981), p. 225; John Hiden and John Farquharson, *Explaining Hitler's Germany: Historians and the Third Reich* (London, 1983), p. 129; Ian Kershaw, *The Nazi Dictatorship: Problems and Perspectives of Interpretation* (London, 1985), p. 151.
32 To date, alternative approaches to the problem addressed by Fischer have not been noted for their superior fecundity. Comparative studies of fascism, for instance, have often gone to the other extreme of trivialising Nazism on the pretext of relativising Hitler. Most practitioners of the 'new social history' have, by definition, manifested little or no interest in these problems, devotees of 'the bitch goddess, quantification', being a conspicuous exception. But a recent evaluation of such methods, as applied to the study of international relations over several decades, concludes that they have produced very modest results and are seriously deficient, even by their own standards – so deficient that the author, himself a quantifier, predicts that 'there will be no major progress in research' along these lines (John A. Vasquez, *The Power of Power Politics: A Critique* (New Brunswick, NJ, 1984), p. 226). See also William Olsen and Nicholas Onuf, 'The growth of a discipline: Reviewed', in Steven Smith (ed.), *International Relations:*

British and American Perspectives (Oxford, 1985), p. 27; Roger Fletcher, 'Germany and the 1914 question: An epilogue to the Fischer thesis', *Teaching History*, vol. 18, no. 4 (1985), pp. 18–21.

33　Georg G. Iggers, 'Federal Republic of Germany', in G. G. Iggers and H. T. Parker (eds), *International Handbook of Historical Studies: Contemporary Research and Theory*, (Westport, Conn., 1979), pp. 217–18. See also Iggers, *The German Conception of History*, rev. edn (Middletown, Conn., 1983).

34　See *Deutsche Historiker*, ed. H.-U. Wehler, 9 vols (Göttingen, 1971–82).

35　Wehler, 'Historiography in Germany today', in Habermas, *Observations*, pp. 225 and 256, n. 28.

36　A. J. P. Taylor, 'Fritz Fischer and his school', *Journal of Modern History*, vol. 47, no. 1 (1975), p. 124.

37　See Thomas S. Kuhn, *The Structure of Scientific Revolutions*, 2nd edn (Chicago, 1970); idem, *The Essential Tension* (Chicago, 1977); D. A. Hollinger, 'T. S. Kuhn's theory of science and its implications for history', *American Historical Review*, vol. 78, no. 2 (1973), pp. 370–93; K. H. Jarausch, 'Illiberalism and beyond: German history in search of a paradigm', *Journal of Modern History*, vol. 55, no. 2 (1983), pp. 268–84. As Jarausch remarks elsewhere, 'The issue is not whether the Kuhnian concept of "paradigm shift" is being correctly applied, but whether the participants understood the development in these terms. On this point the evidence is unanimous.' ('German social history – American style', p. 6, n. 14).

38　See Jörn Rüsen, 'Theory and history in the development of West German historical studies', *German Studies Review*, vol. 7, no. 1 (1984), p. 16.

39　As David Kaiser has observed, 'Fischer himself has been frequently and rightly criticized for merely concatenating discussions of the political and ideological climate of pre-1914 Germany – liberally spiced with quotations from extreme polemicists – with more traditional analyses of the German government's major decisions, while failing to explain exactly how the former influenced the latter' (Kaiser, 'Germany and the origins of the First World War', p. 442).

40　R. G. Moeller, 'The Kaiserreich recast? Continuity and change in modern German historiography', *Journal of Social History*, vol. 17, no. 4 (1984), pp. 655–6. See also Faulenbach, *Ideologie des deutschen Weges*; Evans, 'The myth of Germany's missing revolution', pp. 67–8; Blackbourn and Eley, *Peculiarities*, pp. 2–4.

41　Moeller, 'The Kaiserreich recast?', p. 656.

42　Kaiser, 'Germany and the origins of the First World War', p. 442.

43　See Kaiser, 'Germany and the origins of the First World War', p. 444, n. 5; Moeller, 'The Kaiserreich recast?', pp. 655–6, 672–3, n. 6.

44　See R. J. Evans, 'Introduction: The sociological interpretation of German labour history', in R. J. Evans (ed.), *The German Working Class 1888–1933*, (London, 1982), pp. 15–53; idem, 'The myth of Germany's missing revolution', pp. 67–94. Konrad Jarausch has dubbed them 'sociopolitical revisionists', but this seems excessively vague and imprecise (Jarausch, 'Illiberalism and beyond', p. 282).

45 On the Bielefeld School, see Wehler, 'Historiography', pp. 221–59; Roger Fletcher, 'Recent Developments in West German Historiography: The Bielefeld School and its critics', *German Studies Review*, vol. 7, no. 3 (1984), pp. 451–80; Moeller, 'The Kaiserreich recast?', pp. 655–83; J. N. Retallack, 'Social history with a vengeance? Some reactions to Hans-Ulrich Wehler's "Das Deutsche Kaiserreich"', *German Studies Review*, vol. 7, no. 3 (1984), pp. 423–50; Theodore S. Hamerow, 'Guilt, redemption, and writing German history', *American Historical Review*, vol. 88, no. 1 (1983), pp. 53–72; Iggers, 'Epilogue', *The German Conception of History*, rev. edn, pp. 269–93; idem, *New Directions in European Historiography*, rev. edn (Middletown, Conn., 1984), pp. 80–122; idem, *The Social History of Politics: Critical Perspectives in West German Historiography since 1945* (Leamington Spa, 1986).

46 Wehler, *Modernisierungstheorie und Geschichte* (Göttingen, 1975); idem, *Historische Sozialwissenschaft und Geschichtsschreibung* (Göttingen, 1980); Jürgen Kocka, *Sozialgeschichte: Begriff – Entwicklung – Probleme* (Göttingen, 1977).

47 The *Sonderweg* debate, in particular, has opened deep and painful fissures within the German historical profession. See Horst Möller (ed.), *Deutscher Sonderweg – Mythos oder Realität?* (Munich, 1982); Fletcher, 'Recent developments'; Moeller, 'The Kaiserreich recast?'; Retallack, 'Social history'; Blackbourn and Eley, *Peculiarities*; Alff, *Deutschlands Sonderung von Europa*. Yet this is not just another storm in an academic teacup; it is a live issue with the gravest and widest national and international political implications. See Walter Laqueur, *Germany Today* (London, 1985), pp. 133, 145, 174, 197–8, 209 and *passim*; Wolfgang T. Schlauch, 'West Germany: Reliable partner? Perspectives on recent German–American relations', *German Studies Review*, vol. 8, no. 1 (1985), pp. 107–25.

48 Both are now available in English translation, by Berg Publishers Ltd., as *The German Empire 1871–1918* (1984) and *Facing Total War* (1985) respectively. Wehler's book has proven particularly popular, having now sold over 130,000 copies in several languages.

49 Thus Volker Berghahn – regarded in some quarters as being Bielefeld's principal emissary in Britain – describes those West German tertiary institutions which have responded favourably to the message and method of Bielefeld as 'a very small minority and in political terms they do not wield much influence' (Berghahn, 'West German historiography between continuity and change: Some Cross-Cultural Comparisons', *Daedalus*, vol. 34, no. 2 [1981], p. 256). In the field of international relations, the work of such people as Hildebrand, Hillgruber and G. Schöllgen would seem to corroborate this pessimistic assessment.

50 See Reinhard Rürup (ed.), *Historische Sozialwissenschaft* (Göttingen, 1977); Kocka, *Sozialgeschichte*; idem, 'Theories of Quantification in History', *Social Science History*, vol. 8, no. 4 (1984), pp. 169–78; idem, 'Historisch-anthropologische Fragestellungen – ein Defizit der Historischen Sozialwissenschaft?', in H. Süssmuth (ed.), *Historische Anthropologie* (Göttingen, 1984), pp. 73–83. In his *Kritische Geschichtswissenschaft in*

emanzipatorischer Absicht (Stuttgart, 1973), Dieter Groh demonstrated an early interest in historical anthropology and a strong affinity with the Bielefelders. His empirical work at this point, *Negative Integration und revolutionärer Attentismus: Die deutsche Sozialdemokratie am Vorabend des Ersten Weltkrieges* (Berlin, 1973) was, in focus and approach, barely distinguishable from that of the Bielefelders. Groh, who is a former student of Werner Conze, now holds a chair at the University of Konstanz, but he has produced no major empirical studies since 1973. Theoretically, he has moved to the left, and he now frequently attacks the Bielefelders on ideological and methodological grounds.

51   See Heinrich Best, 'Quantifizierende Historische Sozialforschung in der Bundesrepublik Deutschland', *Geschichte in Köln*, vol. 9 (1981), pp. 121–57; Lutz Niethammer (ed.), *Lebenserfahrung und kollektives Gedächtnis: Die Praxis der Oral History* (Frankfurt, 1980); Süssmuth, 'Historisch-anthropologische Fragestellungen'; *Geschichtsdidaktik*, vol. 9, no. 3 (1984); *Geschichte und Gesellschaft*, vol. 10, no. 3 (1984).

52   See Fletcher, 'Recent developments'; Groh, 'Base processes and the problem of organization: Outline of a social history research project', *Social History*, vol. 4, no. 2 (1979), pp. 265–83; Evans, 'The myth of Germany's missing revolution'; Blackbourn and Eley, *Peculiarities*. In his *New Left Review* article Evans rightly observes (pp. 72–3) that 'the first really serious neo-Marxist critique of the "structural continuity" thesis has been launched from outside Germany, by two British historians, David Blackbourn and Geoff Eley', but he seems to overestimate the real impact he and his comrades have made within Germany. See also Eley, 'Reading Gramsci in English: Observations on the reception of Antonio Gramsci in the English-speaking world 1957–82', *European History Quarterly*, vol. 14, no. 4 (1984), pp. 441–77; Danièle Léger, 'Pour une sociologie marxiste du politique: itinéraire de Nicos Poulantzas', *Revue française de sociologie*, vol. 17, no. 3 (1976), pp. 509–32.

53   R. J. Evans, 'From Hitler to Bismarck: "Third Reich" and Kaiserreich in recent historiography. Part II', *Historical Journal*, vol. 26, no. 4 (1984), p. 1003.

54   They are successfully producing their own journals and other publications, as well as organizing their own conferences and festivals. See the controversy between Detlev Peukert and Alf Lüdtke in *Das Argument*, no. 140 (1983); *Geschichtsdidaktik*, vol. 9, no. 3 (1984) (issue on 'Oral history – Kommunikative Geschichte – "Geschichte von unten"'); *Geschichte und Gesellschaft*, vol. 10, no. 3 (1984) (issue on 'Sozialgeschichte und Kulturanthropologie'); Süssmuth, 'Historisch-anthropologische Fragestellungen'.

55   On the 'new history movement', see 'Ein kräftiger Schub für die Vergangenheit', *Der Spiegel*, vol. 37, no. 23 (6.6.1983), pp. 36–42; Volker Ullrich, 'Alltagsgeschichte: Über einen neuen Trend in der Bundesrepublik', *Neue Politische Literatur*, vol. 29, no. 1 (1984), pp. 50–71; idem, 'Spuren im Alltag', *Die Zeit*, no. 45 (2.11.1984), p. 73; Peter Schöttler, 'Historiker auf neuen Pfaden: Spurensicherung im Alltag', *Frankfurter*

Rundschau, no. 3 (4.1.1984), p. 14; idem, 'Die Geschichtswerkstatt e.V.: Zu einem Versuch, basisdemokratische Geschichtsinitiativen und -forschungen zu "vernetzen"', *Geschichte und Gesellschaft*, vol. 10, no. 3 (1984), pp. 421–4; Alfred Georg Frei, 'Alltag – Region – Politik: Anmerkungen zur "neuen Geschichtsbewegung"', *Geschichtsdidaktik*, vol. 9, no. 2 (1984), pp. 107–20; Hannes Heer and Volker Ullrich (ed.), *Geschichte entdecken: Erfahrungen und Projekte der neuen Geschichtsbewegung* (Reinbek b. Hamburg, 1985); Anthony McElligott, 'The German history workshop festival in Berlin, May–June 1984', *German History*, No. 2 (1985), pp. 21–9; Gert Zank, *Die unaufhaltsame Annäherung an das Einzelne: Reflexionen über den theoretischen und praktischen Nutzen der Regional- und Alltagsgeschichte* (Konstanz, 1985); Gerhard Paul and Bernhard Schossig (eds), *Die andere Geschichte* (Cologne, 1986). On the 'Greens', see Horst Mewes, 'The West German Green Party', *New German Critique*, vol. 28 (1983), pp. 51–85; Laqueur, *Germany Today*, pp. 57–9 and *passim*; Elim Papadakis, *The Green Movement in West Germany* (London, 1984); Fritjof Capra and Charlene Spretnak, *Green Politics* (London, 1984), pp. 3–162.

56 See Jarausch, 'Illiberalism and beyond', p. 284; Michael Grüttner, *Arbeitswelt an der Wasserkante: Sozialgeschichte der Hamburger Hafenarbeiter 1886–1914* (Göttingen, 1984), p. 15.

57 Based at the Max Planck Institute for Historical Research in Göttingen, and, together with Hans Medick, one of the principal anti-Bielefeld gadflies pushing 'history from below' in the form of historical anthropology in particular.

58 See William R. Keylor, *The Twentieth-Century World: An International History* (New York and Oxford, 1984), p. 43.

59 William L. Patch, Jr, 'German social history and labor history: A troubled partnership', *Journal of Modern History*, vol. 56, no. 3 (1984), p. 483. A. J. P. Taylor also refers to 'the revolution in the German historical outlook launched by Fritz Fischer' (Taylor, *A Personal History*, Coronet edn (London, 1984), p. 224).

60 Hamerow, 'Guilt, redemption, and writing German history', p. 71.

61 See Sonja Eichhofer, 'Der 8. Mai 1945 und die geistige Bewältigung der imperialistischen Vergangenheit', *Zeitschrift für Geschichtswissenschaft*, vol. 18, no. 4 (1970), pp. 480–96.

62 Jarausch, *Students, Society, and Politics in Imperial Germany: The Rise of Academic Illiberalism* (Princeton, NJ, 1982), p. 423.

63 James Joll, 'The conquest of the past', *International Affairs*, vol. 40, no. 3 (1964), p. 490.

64 Karl Jaspers, *Wohin treibt die Bundesrepublik?* (Munich, 1966), p. 204. See also Francis Duke, 'Historiography as "Kulturkampf": The Fischer thesis, German democracy and the authoritarian state', *Literature and History*, Spring 1980, pp. 94–110.

65 Fritz K. Ringer, *The Decline of the German Mandarins: The German Academic Community 1890–1933* (Cambridge, Mass., 1969), pp. 2–3;

C. E. McClelland, *The German Historians and England* (Cambridge, 1971), pp. 6, 233, 236; idem, *State, Society, and University in Germany, 1700–1914* (Cambridge, 1980), pp. 322–40; Jarausch, *Students, Society, and Politics*, p. 8 and *passim*; Craig, *The Germans*, p. 173.

66 Craig, *The Germans*, p. 171.

67 Cf. Theodor Adorno, *Erziehung zur Mündigkeit* (Frankfurt, 1970).

68 See Richard Löwenthal, *Gesellschaftswandel und Kulturkrise: Zukunftsprobleme der westlichen Demokratien* (Frankfurt, 1979); Laqueur, *Germany Today*, p. 50. Pessimism is nowadays ubiquitous. Cf. Christopher Lasch, *The Culture of Narcissism* (New York, 1979); Eugene Kamenka, 'A world we do not like', *Quadrant*, vol. 29, no. 8 (1985), pp. 65–6; Petra Kelly, *Fighting for Hope* (London, 1984).

69 Ringer, *The German Mandarins*, p. 446; idem, *Education and Society in Modern Europe*, pp. 7–8, 112; Laqueur, *Germany Today*, pp. 50, 68–74; Craig, *The Germans*, pp. 170–89.

70 Hans Mommsen, 'Die deutschen Eliten', p. 102.

71 V. R. Berghahn, 'Die Fischer-Kontroverse – 15 Jahre danach', *Geschichte und Gesellschaft*, vol. 6, no. 3 (1980), pp. 403–19; idem, 'West German historians between continuity and change', p . 256.

72 Laqueur, *Germany Today*, p. 135.

73 *Ibid.*, p. 224.

74 Jonathan Steinberg, 'The art of Denis Mack Smith', *London Review of Books*, vol. 7, no. 9 (23.5.1985), p. 16.

75 H. T. Wade-Gery, 'Thucydides', N. G. L. Hammond and H. H. Scullard (eds), *Oxford Classical Dictionary*, 2nd edn (Oxford, 1970), p. 1069.

76 See Stephen Van Evera, 'The cult of the offensive and the origins of the First World War', *International Security*, vol. 9, no. 1 (1984), pp. 58–107. If history is really more art than science, as historians from Herodotus and Plutarch to Theodor Mommsen, A. J. P. Taylor and François Furet have believed, we may have much less cause to cavil at Fischer's methodological shortcomings than some of his critics have maintained. See John Hart, *Herodotus and Greek History* (London and New York, 1982); Arnaldo Momigliano, *Essays in Ancient and Modern Historiography* (Oxford, 1977); Ernst Breisach, *Historiography: Ancient, Medieval and Modern* (Chicago and London, 1983); Theodor Mommsen, *Reden und Aufsätze* (Berlin, 1905), pp. 11; Taylor, *A Personal History*, p. 160; François Furet, 'Beyond the *Annales*', *Journal of Modern History*, vol. 55, no. 3 (1983), p. 408.

Foreword to the Anglo-American Edition

After 1945 the historical profession in West Germany concentrated almost exclusively on research into the 'Third Reich' in a manner which facilitated the contemplation of this period as a unique phenomenon, without parallel in the course of German history. From this perspective it was possible to interpret the twelve years of Hitler's Reich, in the terminology of Fritz Stern of Columbia University, as a *Betriebsunfall* (accident or derailment) in recent German history, as the most poignant expression of discontinuity. This view did not begin to be abandoned until the late 1950s and early 1960s, when my own books and articles reopened the debate on German war aims in the First World War. The subsequent controversy directed attention to the problem of continuity in recent German history, a problem to which I referred in the preface of my 1961 book, looking back to Imperial Germany and forward to Weimar and Hitler's Germany. German historians working abroad now started to see this as marking the conclusion of the 'restoration' phase in German historiography and, for the first time, began to perceive the period 1871–1945 as a coherent historical unit. The 75 years of the Prusso-German Empire thus stood out in sharp relief both from Germany prior to 1866–71, the 'Germanic Confederation', and from Germany after 1945–49, revealing these turning-points or upheavals as the most crucial discontinuities, and certainly as being more decisive than the caesuras and watersheds of 1888–90, 1918–19 or 1933.

Thereafter, scholars had the option, methodologically speaking, of demonstrating continuities either in terms of foreign policy and diplomatic traditions and tactics – the practice of Andreas Hillgruber, for example – or by accentuating social and economic structures and the realm of religious and political ideas, as was done by my 'school' and, independently of me, by Hans-Ulrich Wehler and Jürgen Kocka. The present study combines both methods and stresses 'power structures' or the role of 'elites'. Far from reflecting an arbitrary choice from the elements involved in the historical process, this approach mirrors the political, social and economic centre of gravity in the Prusso-German Reich while taking due cognizance of the actions and responses that it prompted within the international system.

Today, Germany's position in the world is a completely different one. The German Reich has ceased to exist. It has been partitioned, one quarter of its former territory being lost forever. The Federal Republic of Germany is a member of the European and Atlantic Western community; the German Democratic Republic is part of Soviet-dominated, Communist Eastern Europe. This is the result of the Second World War. If, as in 1914 and 1939, the status quo were again challenged by violent means, a third global catastrophe would ensue.

But even the internal situation within each of the two German states has altered dramatically. In the East, radical social change has created a centralized and bureaucratic structure. In the West, there was a revival of the liberal-democratic Weimar state in a more mature form. In former times it had been unable to strike root because the traditions of the Bismarckian Reich proved the more powerful. Yet the weighting of social and economic groups and their relationships with one another are also very different today from what they were in Imperial Germany and during the Weimar Republic. In the Federal Republic there are no longer any 'Junkers', in the sense of East Elbian agrarians, and heavy industry based on coal and iron no longer occupies a special position. Today, finishing and export industries take precedence over basic commodity industries. Social Democracy and the trade unions have ceased to be merely tolerated. With their positions securely based in law, they are now among the pillars of political and economic life and, having emancipated themselves from ideology, they have become integrated into the social order. Although the cutting of the cake still produces vehement struggles over wages and profits, the style of political and economic debate has changed because neither side any longer calls into question the social and political order. The defence forces are now subject to the political supervision of the government, are no longer a state within the state, and 'civilian' life has ceased to be militarized. The Federal

President is not the 'ersatz Kaiser' he was under Weimar. Although much of the old has survived, and flourishes still, the new is today the overwhelmingly dominant element.

In forty years a new continuity has thus been established. We are entitled to hope that it will go on growing in strength and durability, unimpaired by the political and economic difficulties which may lie ahead.

Foreword to the German Edition

Continuity, together with its antithesis of discontinuity, is such a general, universal historical category that we shall here confine our observations to a specifically German variation in the very recent modern era.[1] All history moves along a spectrum of continuity and discontinuity, of tradition and novelty. German history is no exception.

The federative tradition of the late medieval German Empire and the post-1815 Germanic Confederation may be seen as representing a more venerable line of continuity. Within this context, liberal-democratic ideas and constitutional usages assumed a place as befitted the age of the bourgeoisie. This tradition was interrupted and partly subsumed by the rise of the Brandenburg-Prussian military state to the position of dominant power in Germany.

After 1866 and 1871, Germany came to experience a more recent line of continuity – that of monarchical-bureaucratic Prussia, which incorporated its military-state tradition into its founding of the German Empire or *Kaiserreich* of 1871.[2] Transcending all political breaks and caesuras, this new continuity retained its dominance, despite modifications and variations in intensity, until 1945, as may be seen from the example of the two world wars. Elements of this more recent continuity may be identified internally and externally: structurally, it was an association of agrarian-aristocratic and industrial/big-bourgeois power elites attempting to maintain their positions against the rising forces of democracy and Social Democracy. Its primarily defensive and conservative domestic purpose was bound up with an expansive and offensive external objective: Prussia's hegemony in Germany was to be followed by the hegemony of Prussia-Germany in Europe, which was to serve as the basis for securing a position of global power as well.

Underlining these characteristic features in the history of the Prusso-German Empire is not an act of arbitrary choice but proceeds rather by inference from the identification of the distribution of political power within the social order and the resulting actions and reactions thereby engendered within the international system. To be sure, continuity does not mean identity, and beside the now dominant strand of continuity there continued to exist after 1866 the older line of continuity of the federative, liberal and democratic element in German life.[3] However, at the peaks of German power, in the *Kaiserreich* and in the 'Third Reich', these traditions were represented by oppositional minorities which were at best tolerated and ultimately discredited and eliminated. Their very existence formed an additional motive for external expansion – on the eve of the First World War, and again in 1933 at the beginning of the 'Third Reich' which culminated in the Second World War.

The relevance of the First World War for the problem of continuity in recent German history raises the question of whether its origin, course, outcome and the whole matter of transcending the war represent a break with the hitherto dominant structures and tendencies or whether these issues bespeak the persistence and longevity of such structures and tendencies. Considered from this angle, the result is fresh and more sharply contoured insights into the existence and persistence of power structures and their underlying consciousness over a period of well-nigh eight decades.

1

Ruling Cartel and Imperialism

'Steel and rye'

The German Empire of 1871 did not stand in the line of continuity emanating from the medieval empire, as the name might suggest, but in that of the state of Brandenburg-Prussia, which the Bavarian historian Karl Alexander von Müller described in August 1914 as an 'heroic-aristocratic warrior state in which everything – taxation, officialdom, economy, society – revolved around the army, was determined by the needs of the army'.[4]

In eighteenth-century Germany this military state was 'an alien phenomenon, incomprehensible to contemporaries'. In the Reform Era it had enhanced its efficiency, at the same time strengthening the position of its ruling caste, the landowning aristocracy. It had defeated the Revolution of 1848, and in the army and constitutional conflict of 1862–6 it had once again repulsed parliamentary government and democracy as well as the subordination of the army to parliamentary control. Indeed, it was the condition of Bismarck's appointment that he maintain undiminished the preponderance of the crown and the army within the state, thus preserving this continuity – though the Olympian dimensions of his personality all but obscured this for two decades. Even the introduction of manhood suffrage for the parliament of the North German Confederation proceeded from an anti-democratic calculation on Bismarck's part. In the Prusso-German Empire, which Bismarck created in three short wars which he 'willed and made',[5] federal elements only thinly disguised the dominance of Prussia, just as the liberal constitutional elements merely served the purpose of masking the dominance of the crown and the aristocracy (holding the leading positions in the army, the high bureaucracy and the diplomatic service) in an age of liberal ascendancy. Thus a pre-industrial elite retained political power as well as control over the chief instrument of power, the army. The latter, via universal conscription and the institution of the 'officer of the reserve',[6] exerted so decisive an influence on the whole society as to permeate all spheres of life with a military spirit of hierarchy and subordination such as the rest of Germany had never before known. School, university and church, above all the Protestant state churches based on Lutheran tradition, with their close association of throne and altar, sanctioned this order: they were in 1848, and again in 1918, anti-revolutionary: the core of the morality which they coined was obedience.[7] Through this habit of subservience, the industrialists' adoption of the 'master in the house' mentality of the estate-holders was greatly facilitated.[8]

In terms of its social ideas and its distribution of political power so monarchic and feudal in structure, this in 1870 still predominantly agrarian German Empire developed in two waves (1850–73 and 1896–1914), and on a scale and tempo bearing comparison only with the development of North America, into a modern industrial state. The new industrial bourgeoisie had established itself as the economically dominant force no later than the onset of the boom period beginning in 1896, but it had been quite unable to acquire for itself a commensurate share in political power. One of the most significant results of Bismarck's conservative policy was his success in reconciling these two social elites by means of his post-1878 economic and social policies, indeed promoting the assimilation of the new industrial big bourgeoisie by the agrarian-feudal forces. This alliance of 'steel and rye', of the manor and the blast furnace,[9] in the fight against Caprivi's reform policy was renewed in Miquel's 'consensus policy' *(Sammlungspolitik)* of 1897–8, cemented through the 1902 Bülow tariff, and in 1913, through the manipulative recruitment of petty-bourgeois groups from the 'old *Mittelstand*', was once again consolidated in the 'cartel of the productive estates'. It persisted as the hard core of reaction within German society and continued to play a decisive role, despite manifold divergences, in 1933. The policy of naval building inaugurated in 1898, although heavy industry (coal, iron and steel) was its chief beneficiary, was yet accepted, albeit with great reluctance, by the agrarians, represented by the Conservatives, because their acquiescence in navalism bought them higher grain tariffs which, in conjunction with direct subsidies, secured their survival as an economic and a social class.

Within industry, whose organizations co-operated closely with the civil service, the heavy industry lobby (the older CDI) consistently outstripped the influence of the BDI (the manufacturing lobby),[10] while the chemical and electrical industries, representing the most advanced of modern technology, were concerned primarily with foreign markets. While finishing industry was more strongly organized in small and medium-sized enterprises, raw-materials industries had already achieved, at a fairly early stage, a high degree of syndication and cartelization (the coal syndicate in 1893, the steel producers' association in 1894). The attempt to strengthen the liberal elements in commerce, banking and industry through the creation of the Hanseatic League in 1909, as an 'anti-feudal consensus policy', proved a failure.[11] 'Latent reform movements' (G. Schmidt) of an 'opening to the left' were not realized;[12] and for the government it was quite impossible to oppose the Conservatives with a centre–left coalition. On the contrary, as late as May 1914 Matthias Erzberger, a leading representative of the Centre Party, could still describe 'the decimation of the gigantic power of Social Democracy' as the greatest task of the Reich's domestic policy, requiring co-operation of the 'right (i.e. the Conservatives), the Centre and the National Liberals'.[13]

Even after the lifting of the anti-Socialist Law the state continued to hound Social Democracy via the civil service and the judiciary.[14] After the turn of the century, however, Social Democracy managed to strengthen its position enormously, at the same time clipping the wings of its social revolutionary faction. Through reformism, the growth of the trade unions and the survival of petty-bourgeois artisan traditions, the party (hitherto a subculture or counter-culture) gradually became assimilated to the existing social order. It was this process of deradicalization which accounted for its decision of 4 August 1914 to vote in favour of war credits. In this embourgeoisement of the party the Hanseatic League saw the possibility of acquiring an ally against the great landowners and heavy industry, which in fact proved unattainable. For the great landowners and heavy industry, together with their lower middle-class and *Bildungsbürgertum* (educated bourgeoisie) supporters, this transformation of Social Democracy and its rise to the position of strongest party in the German Reichstag in January 1912 served as an alarm signal and an occasion to go beyond their anti-democratic animus and to demand that the Reichstag be neutered and the trade unions suppressed, for it seemed to them that their economic and social position could be guaranteed only in an authoritarian corporate state: here the nexus with Papen's ideas of 1932, even with the year 1933, becomes palpable. To them it seemed that external aggrandizement and possibly even victorious war abroad might be the appropriate means for combating the Social Democratic, no less than the liberal-democratic challenge – as had proved expedient in 1866.

In the meantime, the conservative royalism and liberal patriotism of the 1860s had been changed into a new German nationalism marked by *völkisch*-racist, populist and pseudo-democratic features. This new nationalism no longer merely toadied to the powers that be but also attacked the government whenever the authorities seemed to act with insufficient dash either at home or abroad. Examples of this include the petty-bourgeois anti-Semitism of the seventies and eighties; the Farmers' League, with its strongly anti-Semitic and, in part, anti-aristocratic peasant groups; the colonialist movement; and the radical wing of the Navy League, with its many agitators of petty-bourgeois origin. This transformation revealed itself most dramatically in the Pan-German League and its affiliations when, between 1911 and 1914, the animus against the 'weak' government intensified to the point of open criticism of the 'weak' Emperor Wilhelm II and began to depict itself as a radical 'revolution of the right', anticipating and preforming elements that were to become manifest in 1933.

From 'World Policy' to Continental Hegemony

Externally, the Reich was caught in a tightening vice between, on the one hand, initial consolidation of its 1871 position by means of Bismarck's alliance policy and, on the other, pressure from sections of the bourgeoisie for expansion of its colonial empire and penetration of the Near East. The Reich remained burdened with the enmity of France, which it was unable to divert overseas. The attempt to repair its damaged relationship with Russia (strained since 1878) was also unsuccessful, not least because the Conservatives (bound to tsardom by political tradition), through their agrarian interests, aggravated that estrangement at the economic level. This led to the Franco-Russian rapprochement (the 1892 military convention). Nevertheless, in 1897–8 the Imperial government under Wilhelm II, with its vehemently anti-British new men, Bülow and Tirpitz (both demonstrably influenced by the historian Treitschke[15]), decided in favour of naval construction and hence of 'world policy' in the sense of overseas expansion. Of necessity, such a policy threw down the gauntlet to Britain, the third possible Great-Power opponent of global stature. In the Reichstag, this policy drew support from the vast majority of the bourgeois parties, including the Centre. Whether it was primarily the powerful economic interests of heavy industry; or (as has recently been maintained, perhaps in exaggeration of the domestic political motives) a 'social imperialism'[16] which, using the navy as its symbol (as Bismarck had used the army), sought to unify all the bourgeois forces against the Social Democratic peril; or whether it was the ideas of the neo-mercantilists and neo-Rankeans, of the professors recruited for naval propaganda work; or whether it was the influence exerted on the Kaiser and Tirpitz by Mahan's teachings about sea power and world standing – for the Great Power in question, namely Britain, these motives were completely immaterial: it was the fact of naval building which counted. What mattered was that the German Empire had embarked on a course aiming at nothing less than 'parity' with the British world empire, if not more. Thus, at any rate, the then Lord Lieutenant of the province of Brandenburg, von Bethmann Hollweg, described the Kaiser's intentions in 1903:

The first and basic idea [of the Kaiser is] to smash the global position of Britain in favour of Germany. It is for this reason, so the Kaiser is firmly convinced, that we need a navy and, in order to build it, a great deal of money. Since only a very rich country can furnish this, Germany must become rich; hence the encouragement given to industry and the annoyance of rural producers protesting against this policy to save themselves from ruin.[17]

In the eyes of the agrarians it remained the 'ghastly' fleet, which they had accepted only in return for the concession of high agricultural tariffs,[18] though these were never high enough in their estimation. The fleet was to be completed by 1918 or 1920 and to be used as a lever or military instrument. When one recalls that Germany at this time was the strongest land power in Europe, it becomes clear that extensive maritime world-power ambitions of this sort must necessarily transform the balance of power and call into question the European states system. In reality, Britain began to respond to this challenge, through her armaments and her ententes, as early as 1901–2.[19]

Contemplating the self-restraint of the Bismarckian and Caprivi eras with a mixture of pity and contempt, and partly animated by concern that Britain might go over to protectionism and close off her markets, a younger generation of Germans unleashed on all parts of the globe a hectic flurry of activity known as 'world policy', seeking to gain spheres of influence in China, for example, in South America, in Turkey especially, and, above all, additional colonies in Africa and the Pacific. What this amounted to in the consciousness of the nation, among the so-called liberal imperialists in particular, was a redivision of the globe that would more accurately reflect prevailing power relations, i.e. acknowledge the rise of the German Empire, than did the status quo. In practice, this could be attained only by means of war. Even a Cassandra warning against war (Hans Plehn in his study, *German World Policy without War*) drew attention to this nexus when he noted as the consequence of German public opinion's bitterness over the German retreat in the crisis of 1911: 'In the year since the last Moroccan crisis it has become virtually the unanimous feeling of the German nation that the freedom necessary to the implementation of our world policy can be won only through a great European war.'[20]

The gains of all such efforts were disappointingly modest. Yet there is a clear continuity here. For the same objectives which were being pursued and, intermittently, even negotiated with

Britain (at the turn of the century and in the years 1912–14) cropped up again as early as August 1914 as one of the Imperial Colonial Office's peace terms (a German Central Africa), augmented in 1916 by the Imperial Navy Office and the Naval Staff with demands for naval stations in Dakar, on the Azores and the Cape Verde Islands, as well as Malta and Cyprus, which were required to secure the German sea-lanes to South America, Africa and the Pacific.[21] The same aims surfaced again in official documents and maps during the Second World War. In them, the Tirpitz tradition lived on.

After the formation of the Triple Entente such aims had become quite dubious, for the German naval programme had, in the meantime, led to a naval arms race with Britain (this assumed the form and the challenge of attempting to keep pace with British naval construction) and at the same time fundamentally altered the international political position of the Reich through Britain's ententes with Japan (1902), France (1904) and Russia (1907). This was seen as a great diminution in Germany's power and perceived subjectively as 'encirclement'. Underlying the latter concept was the sense of being cut off from future development of the nation's power potential. The financial strains of the naval programme also had the effect of destabilizing rather than stabilizing the domestic political system, for the inevitable financial reform (1909) once again spared the Conservatives while burdening the business classes and the masses.[22] After 1905 the Reich attempted, in a number of major crises, to break out of its 'encirclement', invariably doing so with an eye to the probable domestic ramifications. Its final endeavour led to the First World War. During these crises the Kaiser repeatedly revealed his own weakness. When he again 'caved in' on 28 July 1914 he was pushed aside. In all this, and at the crux of military deliberations from 1908 onwards, there was the anticipated and accepted two-front war with France and Russia. Only the active hostility of the third world power, Britain, remained in doubt.

In the first Moroccan crisis of 1904–5, which was generally regarded in retrospect as the most opportune moment to 'strike' because Russia was then preoccupied in East Asia, France stepped back from the brink. Within the Reich, among its political and military leaders, the Social Democratic threat appeared to reach a climax, while at this juncture neither the army (then undergoing a reconversion in armament) nor the navy seemed ready for a great war. Fear of a recrudescence of the revolutionary events of the year 1848 remained dormant but ever-present during the crises of the seventies (the anti-Socialist Law), the eighties (the miners' strike) and the nineties (the Hamburg dock workers' strike), reaching a new peak with the great 1905 Ruhr miners' strike which was taken all the more seriously because the Russian revolution and its bloody clashes were expected to have repercussions within Germany. After Wilhelm II had proclaimed excitedly in the Prussian council of ministers' meeting of 24 January 1904, 'I am due revenge for [18]48 – revenge!',[23] by late 1905 it had become clear to the Kaiser that:

> because of our Social Democrats we cannot send a single man out of the country without running the gravest risk to the life and property of the citizenry. First the socialists must be gunned down, decapitated and rendered harmless, in a blood-bath if necessary, and then war abroad! But not beforehand and not *à tempo*.[24]

That the forces in the German government pressing for utilization of the favourable external situation were unable to assert themselves was due, in part, to the assumed domestic political threat but also, and more importantly, to the technical condition of the German army, which in the realm of field artillery weaponry was then vastly inferior to the French army, its main opponent. In this sense, the German army was, in fact, virtually unfit for active service. What we have here is a classic instance of a political decision being influenced by deficiencies in military technology. This was still more true of the navy, which in 1905 remained incomplete and could therefore not be exposed to a preventive British strike à la Copenhagen in 1807.

In the Bosnian annexation crisis, in which the Dual Alliance was converted, for the first time, from a defensive association into an acquisitive alliance and the entire German Balkan and Near Eastern policy was at risk, Russia backed down because of her weakened condition following the Japanese war and the 1905 revolution, to say nothing of Britain's manifest lack of interest in her predicament. Even at this point, however, when the monarchical system and its 'power prestige' had been severely shaken by the *Daily Telegraph* affair, the German 'war party' already perceived war as the means of scoring a great external success that would impose with a single blow a lasting roll-back on both the liberal-democratic and the Social Democratic movements – in short, of repeating the experiment of 1866. Thus, at any rate, the situation was understood and described by an experienced observer of the German scene, the Russian ambassador in Berlin, Count Nicolai Osten-Sacken:

> The war party, misled by the undeniable military preparedness of the army and of the other castes in society, offended in its feelings of traditional devotion to the supreme leader, considers war as the sole possible means of restoring to the monarchical power that prestige which has been forfeited in the eyes of the popular masses.
>
> The mood of the military circles draws strength from the conviction that the present temporal superiority of the army promises Germany the greatest chances of success. Such a conviction is capable of seducing this emperor and giving his foreign policy a militant character.
>
> On the other hand, a victorious war could, at least initially, diminish the pressure of radical aspirations among the people for change in both the Prussian and Imperial constitutions in a more liberal sense.[25]

If the German government were sure of the British neutrality which it coveted, then war would begin at once, wrote Osten-Sacken. Bitterness in conservative and military circles over criticism of Wilhelm II by the Reichstag and parts of the press at the time of the *Daily Telegraph* affair was certainly mixed with mistrust of the person of the Kaiser in the event of a military crisis. 'Moltke does not fear the French and the Russians so much as the Kaiser' (because of his weak nerves), so the Chief of the Military Cabinet, General von Lyncker, reported to the Lord Chamberlain, von Zedlitzsch-Trützschler. Russia's retreat before the German semi-ultimatum of April 1909 (in respect of the Bosnian annexation question) prevented this problem from coming to a head until July 1914.

In the second Moroccan crisis of 1911 the German government yielded to British intervention on behalf of France (Lloyd George's Mansion House speech), the more so as its own allies proved uninterested in the matter. However, in the wake of the government's use of the Pan-Germans for agitational purposes, the excitement and bitterness of nationalist opinion over what was seen to be the humiliating outcome of the crisis were profound and enduring. Now the target of pejorative criticism at home and abroad was not only the government of Chancellor Bethmann Hollweg but the person of the emperor as well – *Guillaume le timide*. Apart from the foreign policy and economic factor (Morocco, Central Africa) comprehending a trial of strength with France, indeed with the Entente, what was also at stake in this crisis was an implicit domestic political calculation on the part of the Wilhelmine 'power bloc'. Thus on 26 August 1911 the heavy-industry *Post* saw a war as guaranteeing 'beside the clarification of our precarious political situation' an all-important 'sanitization of many political and social conditions', while the *Armeeblatt* wrote in lapidary style, 'For relations within Germany a grand passage of arms would be not at all a bad thing, even if it means tears and pain for individual families.'[26] When, a little later, in January 1912, Social Democracy emerged as the strongest party in the Reichstag, making the *coup d'état* demanded by the Pan-German Conservatives appear no longer feasible, the anticipated curative internal effects of a war became the focus of still more fervent hopes.

When the surprising collapse of the Reich's Turkish friend in the first Balkan war (October 1912) unleashed a fresh crisis, Britain warned the Berlin government that it would not stand idly by on this occasion, as it had in 1870, should France be overrun by Germany, because it would then confront a hegemonial power in command of the Continent. But this was the very goal which was expressly and repeatedly endorsed not only by the Kaiser – he pictured himself at the head of the 'United States of Europe' – but was seen as self-evident by the military and the widest circles of German bourgeois opinion, many actually regarding it as an existing reality. War was indeed averted by another Russian retreat (as in 1909), but Britain's unmistakable warning did not produce a change in Germany's strategic planning or in her general political style: it led only to an intensified armaments build-up – now exclusively military in character – while the deadline for the allegedly inevitable clash was postponed by one and a half years out of concern for the navy. This was the outcome of the so-called 'war council' of 8 December 1912,[27] to which the Kaiser, excited by the British warning, called his army and navy chiefs. In the Prusso-German Empire, given the position of the military leaders in immediate contact with the monarch, their assessment of the necessity and likelihood of war against two, possibly even three Great Powers carried such weight that the civilian chancellor was in no position to oppose them with political objections, whatever his personal inclination to do so.

There followed what was by 1913 the largest army increase since the creation of the Reich,[28] the Prussian War Minister, and hence the political system, having hitherto kept the army numerically relatively small – out of concern for the maintenance of the aristocratic share of the officer corps and the rural component among the other ranks. Furthermore, a propaganda campaign began against Pan-Slavism, against the Slavic flood threatening the Teuton, but also against the French 'hereditary enemy'. Finally, the Austro-Hungarian ally was restrained until, at the appropriate moment, a Balkan incident should compel it to act in unison with the Reich – in a war in which it had a most important function, namely that of tying down Russian armies until German forces could be thrown against the East.

In the years 1912–14, during which German Near Eastern policy reached its apogee and at once appeared to enter jeopardy, German armaments priority passed from the navy to the army, for it was with the latter, as the great war-scares had made abundantly clear, that the power position of the Reich and the possible outcome of a war were to continue to rest. That is to say, the political fulcrum was transferred from overseas concerns to the bracing of Germany's Continental position in western, eastern and south-eastern Europe. Yet this by no means signified the renunciation of overseas interests. On the contrary, it was assumed that a victory on the Continent, i.e. the enlargement and consolidation of the Reich's European base, would also provide a solution to overseas problems – either through the dead-weight of change in this war or by means of a second 'Punic War'.

Corresponding with the social, economic and military forces within the Reich, this dualism kept in suspense the focal point of German ambitions after the overthrow of France – in the sense of an anti-Western (British) and/or an anti-Eastern (Russian) orientation, a 'both/and' in which the historian G. W. Hallgarten professed to see the cause of the over-reaching of German potentialities.

'Polycratic Chaos' or Military State?

Today it has become fashionable to interpret the origins of the First World War in the July crisis of 1914 as a German death-or-glory gamble born of pessimism and resignation, of 'fear and desperation'.[29] Initiated by Michael Freund, this view has also been extended in continuity to discussions of the origins of the Second World War. Yet it is a construct which finds no support in the sources. Even the Conservatives, who hoped that a war would strengthen the monarchical principle and the existing balance of political forces, acted not from a mood of despair but from the self-awareness of preserving their hereditary position, and hence the prevailing system of domination. Posterity may accuse them of 'autism' and inability to learn, but this has scant bearing on the essential facts. To assert that it was an 'offensively conducted defensive war' is to adopt the vocabulary of the German Foreign Office of 1919, but a critical historical discipline cannot accept such terminology. (During the First World War the thesis was propounded that Germany had been attacked suddenly and treacherously by a hostile coalition.) Putting aside the 'preventive war' question, we may claim as a matter of fact that prior to the First World War war was still regarded as a legitimate instrument of politics. In the words of Zara Steiner, 'When war was considered it was not thought of in modern terms. Except for a few sensitive observers, military action in the old style was a possible extension of diplomacy.'[30] A third approach to German policy in the July crisis draws on the theory of the 'calculated risk',[31] a political science model applicable to crisis diplomacy, such as Kurt Riezler (assistant to Chancellor Bethmann Hollweg) presented in his book *Prolegomena to a Theory of Politics and to Other Theories* (1912) and which the Imperial Chancellor is said to have implemented. And yet in February 1913 during a comparable crisis, when Austria-Hungary was threatening to go to war with Serbia and Montenegro over the question of Albania's frontiers and Bethmann then wanted to restrain his ally in view of the anticipated reorientation of Britain, the same Bethmann Hollweg called attention to the consequences of such a war. The spokesmen of the peace party in St Petersburg, Sazonov and Kokovtsov, so the chancellor wrote, would be 'simply swept away by the storm of public opinion if they should attempt to resist it'. Objective analysis revealed 'that in view of its traditional relations with the Balkan states, it is nearly impossible for Russia to contemplate passively an Austro-Hungarian military action against Serbia without incurring an enormous loss of prestige'.[32] Could the same man have 'forgotten' this insight one year later? He did not. The difference was that he now believed he had Britain more or less where he wanted her. The answer to the risk question was provided by Jagow's deputy, Under Secretary of State for Foreign Affairs Zimmermann, when he said to Count Hoyos in response to Hoyos's inquiry regarding the consequences of a warlike action against Serbia, 'there is a 90 per cent chance that this will mean war with Russia!'[33] Where is the risk element here? One might speak of risk if there had been a 10 per cent or a 20 per cent probability of a major war, but if war was 90 per cent certain one can only conclude that the goal was war itself, and war immediately. Thus Szögyény, the Austro-Hungarian ambassador in Berlin, reported to Berchtold on 12 July 1914:

> The German government considers the present moment to be 'politically optimal' from the German standpoint as well. Russia is 'for the moment inadequately' prepared for war; 'so it is at present a long way from being militarily ready and nowhere near as strong as it probably will be in a few years time'. The German government further believes itself to be in possession of indicators suggesting 'that Britain would not at present participate in a war that broke out because of a Balkan country, not even if it should lead to armed conflict with Russia and possibly also with France'.[34]

The chancellor's task was merely to manage the crisis so that national unity was upheld, i.e. by ensuring Social Democratic compliance. In this he succeeded. On 1 August 1914 Admiral von Müller noted in his diary: 'Atmosphere brilliant, the government has had a lucky hand in being able to depict us as the victims of aggression.'[35] Bethmann Hollweg had simply to await the Russian general mobilization, requiring only the ultimatum to St Petersburg in order to be able to 'stampede' Social Democracy, as he put it, and make his bid to keep Britain neutral, however briefly. In this he was unsuccessful. By contrast with the wavering moments of the Kaiser and the generals, the chancellor had continued – from 8 December 1912 to 4 August 1914 – to cling firmly to the hope that Britain would move away from the Entente.[36] He did so because he believed it possible to influence Grey, via British public opinion and the City, with the notion that Britain's most dangerous competitors were the USA and Japan rather than Germany. In the 1930s Hitler made the very same attempt to neutralize Britain, which again turned out to be illusory.

The *Kaiserreich* was not, as portrayed in some of the more recent literature, a 'polycracy of forces', each paralysing the other so that political decision-making and activity became impossible.[37] W. J. Mommsen, for one, argues from structural-functional premises (supported by Klaus Hildebrand, who also draws on Eckart Kehr's 'primacy of domestic politics' while further availing himself of categories borrowed from traditional diplomatic history) that the Reich was 'ungovernable'. In this analysis an aggressive war was precluded by the very 'warps' in the structure of Wilhelmine Germany: it was impossible by virtue of the 'polycratic trait in the political chaos of the Bethmann Hollweg era'. In reality, there did indeed exist at the summit of the Reich a degree of collaboration between political and military leaders, embracing propagandist and psychological as well as financial and economic preparations for war. A clear decision was made to secure and extend its European base although, with a view to Britain, the timetable, tactics and line of march might vary. And this decision was taken not from a purely military standpoint to secure a Great Power's 'freedom of action' because in 1916–17 French and Russian counter-measures would be complete; it was made from a long-term power-political, economic and domestic political perspective.

The unity of military, political and economic motives is especially clear in the vindication of the 'inevitability' of the 'imminent' war against 'contemporary France', whose destruction was of crucial importance to supporters of both the western and eastern orientations in German imperialism. German industry was annoyed at French resistance to its *'pénétration pacifique'*. Both before and during the war, it considered the ore-basin of Longwy-Briey as the objective that must be acquired.[38] The Kaiser, the Imperial government and the interest groups were embittered that France, of all the powers, should have had the temerity to oppose German economic and political expansion in Turkey. Particularly apposite in this respect is the description given by the Belgian envoy Baron Beyens (after an interview in October 1913 in which the Kaiser and Moltke sought to obtain from King Albert permission for German troops to pass through Belgium) to what he regarded as the 'real' reasons for the bellicose attitude of the Germans:

> Like many of their compatriots, the generals are sick and tired of seeing France asserting herself against Germany in the most thorny of political questions, constantly opposing Germany, involving her in discomfitures, resisting her ascendancy or opposing the hegemonial influence of the German Empire in Europe and her colonial aspirations, repeatedly making desperate efforts to augment her army in order to maintain the balance of forces which, as they believe, has long since ceased to exist in reality.[39]

And only two months later, in January 1914, the chancellor repeated such ideas in a conversation with the French ambassador Cambon when he protested against France's obstruction of German policy in Turkey with the aid of her 'financial weapon':

> Each day Germany sees her population growing immeasurably. Her navy, her industry, her commerce are developing incomparably. She needs 'expansion', she has a claim to a 'place in the sun' . . . If you [French] deny her this, which is the legitimate claim of every living creature, you still cannot impede her growth! But [so Bethmann Hollweg continued]

you will then have Germany as your opponent not only in
Asia Minor but everywhere.[40]

The Social Darwinism manifest in this statement of the German
chancellor, reflecting the way of thinking of his acolyte Kurt
Riezler, can be found a hundred times over in the political
publications of the era. Part of its stock in trade was the idea of the
ineluctable biological and economic growth of the Reich. Another
aspect was the notion of the biological degeneration and economic
decline of France. Yet another ingredient was the image of the
biological and future economic rise of Russia. Social Darwinist
ideas – whatever one might nowadays sometimes read to the
contrary – were therefore by no means peculiar to Hitler. In this
respect the latter was, in fact, very much a product of the pre-First
World War era, as indeed he was in other respects too – for
example, in regard to the idea of the inevitable racial struggle
between Slav and Teuton and the concept of *Lebensraum*, which
was already in common use before the First World War. All these
ideas had a currency that was by no means confined to the
Pan-German movement.

Berlin's misjudgement of British policy was but one of many
illusions afflicting the Imperial government in July 1914,[41] even if
it was undoubtedly the most momentous of these. Perhaps the
German vision had become so clouded by Social Darwinism that
the Reich leaders failed to recognize that what was at stake in 1914
was the 'whole great problem of the European balance'. As a
Swiss observer noted as early as 9 September 1914 in relation to
Britain's attitude, this war was about 'nothing less than the
hegemony of one power in Europe, and hence also a question of
influence in the Mediterranean, the future of the great colonies of
Africa and supremacy over all Asia Minor. Britain was fully
conscious of all this; she knew that Germany's triumph would
mean her diminution, possibly her ruin.'[42] Out of these considerations, and not for the sake of Belgium or because of secret
military obligations, Britain immediately entered the great conflict. This view of the struggle as a global one is reinforced, on the
German side, by Kurt Riezler's interpretation of August 1916,
well before the USA entered the war. From the German view-
point, the 'threefold purpose' of the war was 'defence against
present-day France, preventive war against the Russia of the

future (as such, too late), struggle with Britain for world domination'.[43] The concept of 'world domination', in the specific sense of conflict with Britain for world hegemony, seems to find retrospective corroboration in an address which General Groener delivered to officers of the Army Supreme Command (OHL) in May 1919. Groener condemned what he called the 'unconscious attempt to challenge Britain for mastery of the world' as premature and inadequately prepared and therefore 'bound to fail' because it had been undertaken before 'we had secured our Continental position'.[44] (In his opinion, as his reference to Schlieffen indicates, this should obviously have occurred no later than 1905.) It appears significant that Kurt Riezler used the expression 'world domination' as early as 21 August 1914, when the German *Mitteleuropa* plan was beginning to take shape.[45] Similarly, in December 1915 the German envoy in Copenhagen, Count Brockdorff-Rantzau, later the ambassador in Moscow during the 1920s, forecast as the result of Germany's revolutionization of Russia that victory in the war would go to the Reich and its 'prize' would be 'the first place in the world'.[46] Even if the concept of 'world domination' should certainly not be overvalued, it is nevertheless not methodologically possible to attribute exclusively to Hitler a 1914–18 concept that is associated with a clearly delineated ideation.

The German military leaders' confidence in victory was based on the Moltke-Schlieffen doctrine of the short war, in accordance with the tradition of the wars of 1864, 1866 and 1870.[47] It was dominated by the pre-eminence of operational thought over a realistic assessment of the numerical strength and resources of the opponent and of one's own long-term potentialities. This mode of thought was still characteristic of the German military in 1941. In 1914 it held that the Reich could triumph over superior odds because:

(1) it had the better strategy. In 1905 Schlieffen believed the Grand General Staff to be in possession of the 'secret of victory';

(2) it was superior in leadership, training, tactics and weapons;

(3) its troops had the higher morale. It was thus a question of making use of the moment when the Reich seemed relatively strong, its opponents relatively unprepared.

2

Between Preservation of the System and External Expansion

The Image and the Reality of War

If the war which began on 1 August 1914 had proceeded as planned, namely as a 'short but violent tempest'[48] destroying France and Russia, each in six weeks, then the domestic political system would have been stabilized, in accord with Conservative expectations, in the interest of the ruling elites of crown, military, landed aristocracy, industry and bureaucracy. For an indefinite future Social Democracy would have sunk to a negligible quantity or, by recognizing the military state, i.e. the privileged position of the army within the state, have been transformed into a malleable or conformist party, as desired, for example, by the 'liberal imperialists'.

Externally, the Entente would have been dissolved, thus achieving, as was generally anticipated, a fundamental revolution in European and global power relations. Indeed, this is what lay behind Bethmann Hollweg's so-called 'September programme' (as it is now known), itself drafted in the shadow of an impending military setback. As the 'general aim of the war' the Imperial Chancellor envisaged the provision of 'security for the German Empire to the west and the east for the conceivable future. To this end, France must be so weakened that it can never rise again as a Great Power, Russia must be pushed back from the German frontier as far as possible and its rule over the non-Russian vassal peoples broken.'[49] This meant two things. In the first place, it entailed the elimination of France as a Great Power – militarily, economically, financially – and its incorporation, together with Luxembourg, Belgium and Holland, into a *Mitteleuropa*

56

economic system dominated by German interests.[50] *Mitteleuropa*
was to embrace Austria-Hungary, a Poland severed from Russia,
and possibly other neighbouring states (including Rumania) as
well. This objective was retained throughout the entire war, even
though the course of the war precluded, for the duration, the
incorporation of France from being pursued more actively.
Recent research has revealed that this aim of a Pan-European
market was prosecuted primarily by chemical and electrical
industry, more generally by export-oriented industries. It could
have been realized only in the face of opposition from agrarian
and heavy-industry interests which were more interested in direct
annexations and in upholding a possibly modified protective
tariff system. Inherent in the *Mitteleuropa* endeavours, which
continued to be pursued in numerous conferences until the
autumn of 1918, was a revival of the ideas of Caprivi and the
neo-mercantilists around the turn of the century, as were deliberations, such as those of Walther Rathenau, dating from the
immediate prewar years. At the root of such endeavours lay a
conception of world economic development that was inimical to
the free-trade tradition. At the same time, moreover, German
policy and Chancellor Bethmann Hollweg personally – in case
Britain, too, should be defeated – in October 1914 also planned to
compel Britain by treaty to abide by her free-trade system and not
to adopt protectionism, an eventuality long feared by the Germans. Apart from the French market, the Russian, too, was to be
opened to German industry by a peace treaty that would impose
on the Russians a long-term trade agreement (going well beyond
the 1904 treaty which was already so abhorred in Russia) fixing
Russian industrial tariffs at a low level. But in spite of such
commercial clutching at Britain and overseas, and towards Russia,
the economic consolidation of Central Europe remained the basis
of German policy. In 1915, in the context of the *Mitteleuropa*
conferences, a high official in the Prussian Ministry for Agriculture, State Lands and Forestries named von Falkenhausen gave
expression to the global perspective of the German *Mitteleuropa*
programme. He described it as being:

> to counterpoise to the great, self-contained economic
> entities of the United States, the British and the Russian

empires an equally solid economic bloc of all the European states, or at least those of Central Europe, under German leadership and with the dual purpose of (1) assuring the members of this whole, and Germany in particular, of supremacy over the European market, and (2) of being able to lead into the fray the aggregate economy of allied Europe, as a united force, in the commercial struggle with those world empires over the conditions on which each should be admitted to the other's markets.

This aim was formulated, also in 1915, still more drastically by Schoenebeck, assistant to the Vice Chancellor and Secretary of State for Home Affairs, Clemens von Delbrück, who in his portfolio performed the actual function of an Imperial Economics Minister: it was 'to create a great Central European economic unit that will enable us to maintain our place in the economic struggle for existence among the peoples and prevent us from sinking into economic impotence in the face of the growing solidarity and burgeoning might of the economic superpowers – Great Britain with her colonies, the United States, Russia, Japan with China'.

The 'general aim of the war' was, in the second place, to drive Russia eastwards and to cripple her permanently by separating her 'non-Russian vassal peoples' from her.[51] As early as 6 August 1914 the German Imperial Chancellor, von Bethmann Hollweg, personally described the object of the war as 'the liberation and military protection of the peoples *(Stämme)* oppressed by Russia, the repulse of Russian despotism back to Moscow'. By the outbreak of war the Caucasus and Finland and, above all, Poland and the Ukraine had already appeared in the files of the Foreign Office and the Imperial Chancellery. On 11 August 1914 Bethmann Hollweg and Foreign Secretary von Jagow emphasized to von Tschirschky, the German ambassador in Vienna, how very important it was that insurgency be promoted in the Ukraine, no less than in Poland – partly as a weapon in the struggle with Russia, and partly because, if the war went well, this would facilitate the creation of buffer states between Russia and Germany or Austria-Hungary, such states being desirable as means of relieving the pressure of the Russian colossus on western Europe and driving Russia as far as possible to the east. As early

as mid-August 1914 the Foreign Office therefore began to support the 'League for the Liberation of the Ukraine', a group of
Ukrainian emigrants of a social revolutionary disposition. In like
manner the Uniate Church and its archbishop in Lemberg were
recruited and supported for liberationist agitation. The Viennese
government also saw as its 'principal objective the greatest possible weakening of Russia' and hence 'the liberation of the Ukraine
and other adjacent peoples oppressed by Russia . . . through the
foundation of an independent Ukrainian state'. For the rest,
Jagow's greatest worry in August 1914 was how a revived Poland
was to be prevented from becoming a crown possession of
Austria-Hungary and to be bound to Prussia-Germany instead,
as was to happen to Belgium in the west. This remained a bone of
contention between the two allies until the end of the war. In this
context, the Army Supreme Command under Hindenburg and
Ludendorff (the third OHL) even envisaged a future war with the
Habsburg Empire if Poland should fall to Austria-Hungary
because this empire would then have become a Slavic state,
clamping an eastern vice on Prussia-Germany. The idea of liberating the non-Russian nationalities was Bethmann Hollweg's most
individual conception, a marked contrast with the annexationist
paroxysm of the Pan-Germans. On 1 September 1914 the Baltic
German Johannes Haller, professor of history at Tübingen and
influential during the Weimar Republic because of his book *The
Epochs of German History*, recorded his agreement with the aims
of the Imperial government:

> Russia must be rendered innocuous, and in order that it
> become so its western provinces, the territory of its foreign
> peoples . . . and above all its seaboards must be forfeit. It
> was through their annexation that Russia became a Great
> Power; with their loss, and that of Finland, Lithuania,
> Poland, Little Russia (i.e., the Ukraine), Bessarabia and the
> Black Sea coast, it will cease to be a Great Power and revert
> to what it was before Peter the Great.[52]

We must compel Russia to cede these territories, for 'then at last',
said Haller, 'will be lifted from us the incubus under which even
Frederick the Great sighed'. Here Haller employed the expression

'incubus' to be 'lifted from us' which Bethmann Hollweg and Jagow used again and again during the war when vindicating their persistently espoused policy of disjoining border states.[53] In 1915 and 1916 Bethmann Hollweg repeatedly proclaimed the same goal in public speeches in the Reichstag, announcing it as a political and moral duty of Germany to 'liberate' from the Muscovite yoke the non-Russian nationalities. He did so, in part, with an eye to US President Wilson and British liberal public opinion. Here he could count on the concurrence of the German left liberals, the Catholics and part of the Social Democrats, while the Conservatives, like the OHL, showed greater interest in direct annexations, such as the so-called 'Polish frontier strip', and in Courland and Livonia. This idea of weakening Russia by detaching the non-Russian nationalities was something Bethmann Hollweg had inherited from his grandfather, Moritz August von Bethmann Hollweg, who had publicly championed it in the *Preussisches Wochenblatt* during the Crimean War, when he sought to lead Prussia to the side of Britain and France against Russia. With the object of reminding the grandson of his 'commission', the Pan-Germans published the substance of these essays in 1915.[54] When, on 23 January 1918, Jagow's second successor Kühlmann presented to the Reichstag party leaders a defence of the third OHL's eastern policy, which culminated in the Peace of Brest-Litovsk, as the continuation of the policy introduced by Bethmann Hollweg, he was thoroughly justified in so doing.[55] The fulfilment of this 1914 objective, briefly realized in 1918, would have effectively moved the German military frontier far to the east, setting up a virtual glacis of satellite states that would have been fully comparable with the belt of states now dominated by the Soviet Union (including the Baltic states recovered by her in 1940). The German system would have differed only in direction and scale, as it would also have incorporated the Ottoman Empire in addition to the Ukraine and the Caucasus. This continuously pursued (against the 'Russian colossus') aim of 1914 or 1914–18 should deter us from attributing authorship of such ideas, and the repeatedly quoted passage on the drive to the east, to the writer of a book penned ten years later, Adolf Hitler. Particularly should it give pause to those who trace the decision of June 1941 back to this book.

In August 1914 the war ran not only, as expected, against France and Russia but also, and contrary to expectations, against Britain. And so the principal currents of German imperialism – the older overseas tendency and the more recent but invariably present, in however dormant a form, Continental stream – met in head-on collision. For Bethmann Hollweg, Jagow and Moltke, Russia was the main enemy. Since victory over France was the precondition for the clash with Russia, France was to be treated with relative mildness. Bethmann Hollweg's idea was to form, together with France and Britain, a West European 'cultural bloc' against Russia.[56] This was opposed by Tirpitz and the economic interests allied with him.[57] In their estimate, Britain was the principal foe of the German Empire, and for this reason Tirpitz regarded the possession of the channel coastline as the ultimate objective in the west. The same view was held by Krupp, who believed, contrary to all historical experience, 'we would here be at the spinal cord of British world supremacy, a position, perhaps the only position, that could bring us lasting amity with Britain'.[58] Following the collapse of all hopes of British neutrality, or that Britain might wage a mere 'phoney war', the Imperial Chancellor came to see the war against Britain as a bitter necessity. In his Reichstag speech of 4 August 1914 he had declared Russia chiefly responsible for the war; in December 1914 he hurled at Britain the charge of being its main instigator, thereby fanning the flames of popular Anglophobia in Germany, already ablaze because of the alleged 'racial treason' of the Anglo-Saxons. Tirpitz's attitude was determined primarily by naval considerations. These inclined him to see the present war as deciding matters of 'global industrial and commercial power' even though the German navy was not yet technically prepared for a struggle of this magnitude. Thus originated the conflict between Bethmann Hollweg and Tirpitz. While the chancellor held back the uncompleted navy, with initial concurrence from Tirpitz, so that 'Britain cannot deprive us of the fruits of our victories over France and Russia',[59] Tirpitz was worried that the army might, in its triumphal progress, decide the war by itself and that for want of naval successes the nation might lose interest in the futher development of the navy after the peace. On 30 August 1914 the Secretary of State for the Navy therefore urged that the fleet be sent into action so that, as he put it, the navy might at least have fought gloriously, if not victoriously. Only in this way would it begin to dawn on the nation that 'we must have a fleet of equal strength to the Royal Navy, although this natural and singular goal could not be articulated during the last two decades'.[60] In this way Tirpitz revealed, if only to close colleagues, his true long-range objective. Bethmann Hollweg prevented the immediate use of the High Seas Fleet in order to have it on hand as a bargaining chip at the peace table, especially since he hoped to be able, with the aid of the 'war levy' to be squeezed from France, to expand the navy to the appropriate level, in case it should come to this, for the current war or for a 'Second Punic War'. What the antagonism between Bethmann Hollweg and Tirpitz revealed was the existence of contrasting options within German policy as well as divergent assessments of the bases of a future German world-power position. Yet the navy was unable to fulfill the expectations held of it or the promises which it made. The subsequent Reich Chancellor Hitler undoubtedly belonged in the tradition of Bethmann Hollweg, Moltke and later Ludendorff. By comparison with their concentration on the Continent, the Tirpitz tradition supported by the navy and Raeder was able to maintain itself only as a 'second eleven' that would be brought into play only after the destruction of Russia.

The Illusions Remain

Everything assumed a different aspect after the lost battle of the Marne and the heavy defeat of the Austrians in Galicia. The expectations of the 'fruits' of victory over France and Russia collapsed with the failure of the German attack before Paris in mid-September 1914, to be finally abandoned with the failure of the German offensives in Flanders, at Langemarck. It is open to question whether the idea of eliminating France with one blow was a realistic one. Even if the question is answered in the negative, the crucial facts are that the German military and political leaders considered it possible and that both the outcome of the entire war and the realization of German war aims were dependent on this decision. Also worthy of consideration is the fact that it was a war of coalitions after the London Agreement of

5 September 1914 converted the loose Entente into a wartime alliance precluding a separate peace. It should further be borne in mind that the real resources of the Allies exceeded those of the Germans, particularly if Italy and the USA were counted as being in the enemy camp, which the Germans did not reckon with prior to 1914 because the one was regarded as an ally while the other was deemed a friendly neutral. Soviet research sees this as the factor which ultimately decided the war. For the purposes of this investigation, however, we are concerned exclusively with German expectations and the German image of war prior to the outbreak of the conflict. It is true, no doubt, that a line of continuity can nevertheless be traced to the Second World War in that here, under very similar circumstances, the problem of these decisive military factors again presented itself.

In the autumn of 1914 the new Chief of the General Staff-cum-War Minister Falkenhayn told the Reichstag deputy Erzberger that after the battle of the Marne the war was 'actually lost'.[61] In early December, in a discussion with the Imperial Chancellor, he called the German army 'a ruined instrument'. In fact, the army had lost 50 per cent of its complement and, following its heavy losses in the officer corps and cadres, was effectively recast as a 'militia army', as the official history of the First World War edited by the Imperial Archives noted at the close of 1914. With each passing day, the war conceived as a 'Blitzkrieg' and designed to last for two campaigns turned into a war of attrition in which the limits of German material and manpower resources began to tell. This transformation was not made known to the German people, overwhelmed as it was by the euphoria of the outbreak of the war and the initial successes in Belgium and France, by Tannenberg and U-boat 9. Indeed, the change was deliberately concealed through manipulation of military bulletins and by the Imperial Chancellor's decision, taken against the conviction of Falkenhayn, to allow no public reference to it for fear of precipitating a collapse in the morale of the German people. If at this juncture, as Karl Heinz Janssen maintains, the war was objectively lost, the point was not grasped even by those Germans at the head of public affairs, or if they did see the truth they were unwilling to draw the appropriate inferences. In reality, such an admission and its consequences might well have resulted in the collapse of the political system from within. What happened, on the contrary, was that the war-aims demands (dating from the very first days of the war) of politicians and interest groups, the Pan-German League among them, and despite the ban on public discussion of this matter, reached a peak in the summer of 1915 in the memorials of the six economic interest groups and in the so-called petitions of the intellectuals. From 1915 to 1917 the German professoriate, whose numerous publications had provided the war with a rationale in the 'ideas of 1914',[62] having denounced Russian despotism and (still more shrilly) the Jacobin and commercial West, and having embraced even Prusso-German 'militarism' against the charges of world opinion over the Belgian 'atrocities', now in their vast majority espoused the most far-reaching war aims of all.

All this transcended personalities. Analysis of the war-aims programmes jointly developed by the two pillars of the conservative Prusso-German system, industry and agriculture,[63] reveals the dualism of the cast of mind and the specific interests of these dominant groups. The representatives of *industry*, people like Krupp, Stinnes, Thyssen, Hugenberg, Roetger and their parliamentary lobby in the Reichstag and the Prussian diet, men such as Erzberger, Stresemann and Bassermann, vied with one another in securing the desired gains – in France through annexation of Longwy-Briey and the acquisition of the whole of the French market, in Luxembourg and Belgium, in the Ukraine and the Transcaucasus, in Rumania, in what was to be left of Russia, as well as in Turkey and, not least, in the anticipated additional colonial acquisitions. To *agriculture*, in return, they were prepared to concede large tracts of eastern Europe. The 'Polish frontier strip', Lithuania, Courland, Livonia, Estonia and possibly White Russia were to be dominated by the Reich either indirectly or by means of direct annexation. Both in a trade treaty to be imposed on a defeated Russia and in the treaties with an independent Poland and Lithuania the unrestricted admission of seasonal rural labour formed an important provision. Added to this was the duty-free admission of German manufactures to the whole of the territory of each respective country, together with the unhindered export of raw materials from each. Moreover, 'internal colonisation', believed to be a threat to the great estates, was to be diverted to the eastern forefield of the Reich through the acquisition of land for the voluntary resettlement of small farmers and war veterans. This was to yield the additional advantage of simultaneously broadening that 'state-preserving' and prolific class which might serve as a counterweight to urbanization and to the inevitable growth in the industrial workforce as industrialization advanced. Leading experts in German agricultural science and in eastern migration were engaged to realize plans for new 'living-space' in the north-east, in 'New Germany' as it was then called. The Ukraine, too, was considered as an important potential supplier of raw materials for industry, indicating that Hitler's utterance to Carl Burckhardt in 1939, 'I must have the Ukraine', was again anything but a novel idea. Furthermore, even during the First World War the *Lebensraum* plans were also a goal of Imperial policy (in 1919, under changed circumstances, they were still being pursued in Latvia by August Winnig and still kept alive by the 'Baltic volunteers' after their return); they were therefore not at all an original invention of Hitler's. Certainly, there was, as yet, no talk of subjugating the Russians as helots. Yet they were feared by virtue of their numerical superiority, although they were considered still undeveloped (by Moltke, for example) and the Estonians and Latvians were defamed (by Otto Dibelius) as 'indolent and uncivilised'. A pinnacle of German cultural interest was the reopening of Dorpat University as a German university as early as September 1918. A Germanizing of both these territories appeared possible.[64] The feasibility of such ideas may seem doubtful; their political wisdom, still more so.

Here there is a discernible gulf between illusion and reality, a continuity of error pointing back to Wilhelmine 'world policy'.[65] Even the decision in favour of unrestricted U-boat warfare, in which it fell to the Centre to occupy the key position in the parliamentary discussion, and during which the entry of the USA into the war was intentionally risked, was characterized by a crass underestimation of the possible military strength of this power, and still more of its political and economic clout – a miscalculation which found its analogue in the Second World War. The voices of luminaries of German historical and philological scholarship, such as Eduard Meyer and Ulrich von Wilamowitz-Möllendorf, vied in this regard with spokesmen of the army and navy over the efficacy of the U-boat and the repercussions of a possible American entry into the war, which was finally to decide the war against Germany. Thus, with typical grandiloquence, Hindenburg was able to say, 'we are armed against all eventualities, against America, Denmark, Holland and even against Switzerland'. Tirpitz's successor Capelle asserted that American troop transports would be sunk by German U-boats: 'So, militarily, America amounts to zero, a complete and absolute nothing, a less than nothing!'[66]

The miscarriage of the war plan in September and its final bankruptcy in November 1914 meant strategically the continuation of the struggle as a 'war of stopgap measures' and, in foreign policy terms, the attempt to conclude a separate peace either with France or with Russia. The latter was demanded by Falkenhayn, also at the insistence of Tirpitz. That meant attempting to terminate the struggle with one side in order to be able, at the very least, to force a victorious and dictated peace on the other. The Imperial Chancellor explained:

> Since we have not succeeded in crushing France in the initial phase of the war . . . even I must doubt that a military defeat of our opponents is still possible as long as the Triple Entente holds together . . . what we could do, if fortune favours us, is to so wear down *France* militarily that she is obliged to accept whatever peace we choose, while at the same time – provided the navy holds, as it promises to do – imposing our will on *Britain*. At the cost of reverting to a kind of *status quo ante* in respect of *Russia*, we could thus still create a favourable set of circumstances in the west. In this way the Triple Entente would be swept aside.[67]

This had nothing whatever to do with an abstract desire for peace. Indeed, just as the Belgian question stood in the way of a settlement with France, even in the case of Russia the so-called security-frontier strip objective (Poland and the 'liberation' of the non-Russian nationalities) stood in the way of bids for a separate peace, in so far as the matter depended on Germany. In any event, as already noted, the Entente had meanwhile become a wartime coalition which forbade a separate peace.

'War Socialism' without Reform

With the foundering of German military operations in September and November 1914 began the war of attrition that was to go on for another four long years – the 'world war' mirrored in the schoolbooks and subsequently analysed as the model of future wars. In military terms, what now commenced was a positional war or war of matériel. Hence the stepped-up production in war industries, the introduction of wartime controls on raw materials and foodstuffs, and state direction of production and the labour market. In a word, there now materialized what was known as 'war socialism', with its numerous semi-governmental war corporations going well beyond prewar moves towards the 'interventionist state'. This wartime supply system was enormously broad in its ramifications and begat a prodigious quasi-governmental bureaucracy which proved ultimately constricting to business and, in particular, to farmers, while providing little benefit to the bulk of the population. Yet these were improvisations conceived in a state of emergency and did not alter the system, i.e. the entrepreneurial system of private capitalism, especially since the latter found its security protected by the traditionalist authoritarian state. In contrast with the interpretations of Kocka and Zunkel, which suggest that such changes were of a structural nature,[68] I would emphasize the persistence factor. Entrepreneurs' relative dissatisfaction with the state should not be equated with a general readiness to change the system, for this did not exist. Widely discussed plans for a 'social economy' must therefore not be over-estimated. Industry and commerce both pressed for this quasi-governmental system of war corporations to be dismantled as quickly as possible, perhaps after a brief period of 'transitional economy'. If this system tended to strengthen revolutionary proclivities within the workforce, it is highly improbable that these would have amounted to anything but for the impending defeat and finally the plea for an armistice, particularly since the authorities succeeded in diverting part of the unrest against 'war profiteers', in which process anti-Semitism was used as a manipulative device.

As early as 1914 and 1915 the unexpectedly long duration of the war led to at least verbal concessions to labour in the form of the so-called 'new-orientation'. As an expression of the future political hopes thus aroused, one might consider the symposium edited by Friedrich Thimme and Carl Legien, *Labour in the New Germany*,[69] in which social reformist professors, representatives of the right wing of Social Democracy and trade-union spokesmen proffered their political suggestions. Yet even this moderate and relatively modest proclamation of postwar co-operation between labour and the state, promising also a continuation of social welfare policies, created alarm in conservative quarters and strengthened their opposition to the Bethmann Hollweg government.

The appointment of the third OHL of Hindenburg and Ludendorff during the great crisis of the war in 1916 (the battles of Verdun and the Somme) led to the attempt to effect a total mobilization of all manpower and economic resources, providing the prototype for the twenties' and thirties' theory of 'total war'. This latest phase in war leadership revealed an army–labour partnership of such intensity and hitherto unknown intimacy, transcending the organization of the war economy in the so-called Hindenburg programme, as to include even deliberate psychological influencing of the masses (for instance, the introduction of patriotic instruction at the front in 1917, and the recourse to so-called home propaganda). In the implementation of this programme concessions were made to the trade unions (in their capacity as guarantors of the loyalty of the masses) through the introduction, in late 1916, of the so-called auxiliary service law which greatly strengthened the trade unions' legal position.[70] This tactical concession dictated by the requirements of war was regarded by the more authoritarian element in industry as much too generous and dangerously close to being irreversible. The auxiliary service law was in part resisted and in part evaded. Looking back in 1932, and speaking on behalf of many, a heavy-industry spokesman could still say that Germany's misfortune had begun in November 1916 with the recognition of the legal position of the trade unions and that this situation could be rectified only through their destruction – which soon followed.

By comparison with such social-policy measures, the general political concessions of the spring and summer of 1917 (such as the promise, made under the impression of the February Revolution in Russia, to abolish the three-class suffrage in Prussia) naturally appeared far more alarming still. In reaction to them, the growing consolidation of the diehard *borussisch* authoritarian camp led not only to the fall of Chancellor Bethmann Hollweg but disclosed qualitatively new forms of mass mobilization on the right. The struggle between supporters of a 'victor's peace' and those of a 'compromise peace' now became synonymous with a struggle between the supporters of the existing system and the weaker group of reformists. The 'Fatherland Party' founded in autumn 1917 in response to the majority parties' 'peace resolution' already revealed unmistakably 'pre-fascist' traits in the sense of an extra-parliamentary *'Sammlung'* (consensus) and non-partisan 'unity party'. Its object was to provide a plebiscitary basis to the *de facto* dictatorship of Hindenburg and Ludendorff. With over a million members, mostly from the lower middle classes, it overtook the mass party of Social Democracy and attempted to penetrate the workforce by founding workers' committees in order to form a counterweight to 'Marxism', to Social Democracy and the Free (socialist) Trade Unions. At the head of one such committee ('for a good German peace') in Munich was Anton Drexler, the subsequent founder of the 'German Workers' Party', which gave birth to the NSDAP or Nazi Party. In common with the older Pan-German League, the Fatherland Party was not in principle anti-Semitic, but anti-Semitic propaganda became a definite admixture to its agitation in the countryside and among the industrial workforce. Yet it never managed to win a significant following among the urban workers. Compared with the later Hitler movement, the Fatherland Party as a new movement remained fixed on an older model; its leadership was recruited predominantly from the traditional upper strata, with a high proportion of Protestant clergy; its political norms were still cast in the mould of the traditionalist authoritarian state; and it made no use, as Hitler did, of the manipulative appeal of anti-capitalist agitation. In the realm of foreign policy, the programme of the Fatherland Party once again signalled unbroken adherence to the now familiar aims in both the east and the west.

Following the October Revolution in Russia, to which the German government's policy of fostering revolution had contributed significantly (Lenin's 'sealed train', for example), the peace settlements with Russia and the Ukraine at Brest-Litovsk and the peace with Rumania at Bucharest gave Germany that objective in the *east* which had been aspired to since 1914. If Ludendorff prized the Ukraine primarily as a means of securing the supply of raw materials and foodstuffs so that the war in the west might be brought to a successful conclusion and the British world empire then tackled in earnest, in the eyes of the Foreign Office, the Imperial Ministry for Commerce and the economy generally the Ukraine and the Caucasus were part of that bordering-states policy whose object was to weaken Russia permanently and to bolster the economic basis of the German Empire in the long term.[71] For this reason the German leaders assembled on the spot a group of prominent experts who, in collaboration with General Groener, were to develop the Ukraine into an independent allied state or into a 'spring board' from which an all-Russian confederation might be penetrated. Via Skoropadsky, the man appointed hetman of the Ukraine, who became a co-founder of the *Völkischer Beobachter* in Munich after the war, this eastern policy was passed on directly to Hitler, who in 1926, in the second volume of his book *Mein Kampf*, proclaimed the goal of re-acquiring the Ukraine, and in 1941 he actually realized it for a time.

The OHL's decision in the spring of 1918, after Russia left the war, to try for victory in the *west* through a last great offensive reawakened the most extravagant expectations in the whole of bourgeois Germany during the months of March to May 1918. Had this offensive succeeded, all the evidence suggests that the war aims laid down in 1914 for Continental Western and Central Europe would have been implemented, and the Western Powers and America would have been compelled to accept the power position gained by the Reich in the east. Consideration for the masses now seemed no longer necessary.[72] The National Liberals walked out of the Reichstag's inter-party parliamentary committee, Stresemann declaring, 'Never has our policy been more favourably situated than at present. We are poised to strike the final blow.' On 2 May 1918 the two Conservative parties in the Prussian House of Representatives, possessing a majority by virtue of the three-class suffrage, defeated the government's bill (and thus also the publicly avowed will of their king and emperor) to introduce the equal suffrage, and the party leader von Heydebrand openly stated that it was a question of power, rejecting electoral equality as unacceptable because 'the decisive importance of the undifferentiated masses, especially the labourers of the cities and the industrial centres', would then be anchored in law. What would happen if 120 to 130 Social Democrats got into the House of Representatives was: taxes would be fixed by the propertyless classes and the propertied would have to pay them. As later on in 1945, faith in miracle weapons became common, and again there was talk of 'world domination'. To combat foreign propaganda and the exhausting effects of the war, a massive propaganda campaign was launched at the front and at home. This was not, it is true, co-ordinated, as Ludendorff demanded, by an 'Imperial Office for Public Enlightenment' that would have been comparable to the subsequent Goebbels ministry of 1933, but a comprehensive 'Central Office for Publicity and Public Instruction' was set up, under Ludendorff's political counsellor von Haeften, for this purpose. As in 1914 and 1915, so it was again in 1917 and 1918 the Protestant churches and their representatives who stood in the firing line of this campaign. Thus Otto Dibelius on the question of peace in 1918: 'The answer is no! Not renunciation and accommodation but utilisation of our power to the utmost – this is the challenge of Christianity, the peace terms that it demands of us German Christians.' After hailing, affirmatively, the peace of Brest-Litovsk as a truce of God, Dibelius said the following during a sermon intended to strengthen confidence for the spring offensive: 'What God has begun he also completes; he does nothing by half. Confidently, we look toward the impending consummation in the west; and it seems to us to be a sacrilege not to trust in God to provide this consummation.' How was a society stamped by such thinking to come to terms with the defeat of 1918? This was repressed and attributed to the failure of the people to fulfil God's commission to the Germans. In October 1918 Protestant theologians were the first to formulate, against the cabinet of Prince Max of Baden, the 'stab in the back legend' and to proclaim it as a case of the fighting troops being let down by the home front.[73]

This notion is a crass distortion of historical truth, for it was not the 'collapse' which followed the revolution but the revolution which was a result of the defeat. What it overlooked was that the allies of Germany – Turkey, Bulgaria and Austria-Hungary – had collapsed well before the internal disorders in the Reich and had granted the Entente the right to pass through their countries. It was equally overlooked that the American army was growing stronger every month while the manpower and material resources of the Reich were exhausted. To have been cheated of victory by traitors! Here was a notion that was to have world-historical consequences through its impact on the ideas of Hitler: it became his trauma. But only because he shared it with millions was he later able, by promising that there would never again be a repetition of 9 November 1918, to seduce and fanaticize these millions. Yet the primary question facing the historian is not the individual and social psychology of this trauma but who invented the stab-in-the-back legend which gave rise to the trauma, who derived benefit from it, and by whom it was disseminated. It was the pillars of the *Kaiserreich* (the army, bureaucracy, industry, the churches and universities) who, with the aid of the press, sermons, memoirs, lawsuits on trumped-up issues and the historical profession (particularly official historiography), created this legend in order to distract attention from the locus of responsibility for the war and the military defeat, and to place the burden of these on Jews and Social Democrats. In October 1918 the chairman of the Pan-German League, Class, called for a 'spirited nationalist party' to wage a 'resolute struggle against Jewry', against whom the 'legitimate anger of the people must be diverted'.[74] In this manner such groups proposed to rescue their position in state and society and to slander the republic as one of 'November criminals', and in this they succeeded. In a similar manner a twenty-year campaign was directed against the so-called 'war-guilt lie', which prevented a rational and critical study of the roots of German prewar and wartime policy, rendering impossible the inevitable distancing of the republic from the *Kaiserreich*.

It was a no less gross misrepresentation of the historical facts when in late November 1918 the then Major Beck, later Hitler's Chief of the General Staff and a major promoter of German rearmament, spoke of the 'cowardly' attack by the revolution against the rear of the fighting forces 'during the most difficult moment of the war' – as if the war might still have been won. What also played a part here was shock at the realization that the political status of the officer corps had been severely shaken, undermining the position of an Imperial elite which regarded itself as the core of the Prusso-German state. To von Manstein, later one of Hitler's field marshals, the events of the revolution appeared as 'the end of the world'.[75] This reaction to the Kaiser's abdication and flight demonstrates that the domestic transformation that began as a consequence of defeat was perceived as being far more drastic and threatening than defeat itself. Not the least of the reasons why this was driven from the conscious mind was the determination to conserve the prestige of the officer corps and the General Staff, together with the myth of the state tradition and all the imponderables associated with the ideal of the military state. But even here the disenchantment occasioned by the outcome of the war could gain expression in harsh criticism of the person of the monarch and of the German people. Thus Vice Admiral Hopmann wrote on 6 October 1918:

> The sins committed by Germany over the last three decades must be atoned for. She was politically mesmerised by blind trust, by slavish subordination to the will of a conceited fool puffed up with vanity . . . We merely played like children in illusions and self-deceit.[76]

However, Hopmann's hope that German political life would in future exhibit greater maturity was not to be fulfilled.

The armistice and the Versailles Treaty, together with their repercussions, were simply blamed on the weakness of the Weimar Republic rather than recognized as the result of the politics of Imperial Germany and the lost war.

3

Tradition versus Democracy

'Authoritarian Capitalism'

The military collapse and the revolutionary disturbances created only superficial caesuras, for the First World War had brought about no qualitative change in the composition of society and the economy. Now as before, the principle of the continuity of that which is continued to hold sway. This applied with particular force to the ruling elites of the *Kaiserreich*: landed property, industry, the army, the *Bildungsbürgertum*, the bureaucracy and the judiciary still occupied their traditional places.[77] Nothing changed as a result of the constitutional revision of the Bismarckian state in October 1918, such measures – instituted at the behest of Ludendorff – being in principle entirely consonant with the tradition of 'revolution from above'. The incipient parliamentarization of the national constitution actually owed much less to indigenous liberal forces than to the demands of US President Wilson, for a show of deference to these, it was hoped, might help the Reich to secure a more advantageous peace. When this expectation was not fulfilled, the German Democratic Party (DDP) declined rapidly from 75 Reichstag seats in January 1919 to a mere two seats by 1933. Liberal-democratic forces remained a weak influence in German society. Thus the German People's Party (DVP) began and ended on the right of the political spectrum after a difficult middle course during the Stresemann years, finally lapsing into insignificance. Despite the swing towards parliamentary democracy that began with the constituent assembly, traditional power structures were not altered, not even by the fall of the monarchy in the Reich and the associated states. Indeed, they tended to be rather strengthened and in part restored in the course of the suppression of the

74

left-wing extremist rebel movements. Thanks to Max Weber, an emphatically monarchistic element lived on in the position of the Reich president, with his emergency powers. Its second incumbent, Hindenburg, the First World War field marshal and victor of Tannenberg, powerfully embodied this element as a kind of 'surrogate emperor', aiding and abetting Hitler's 'seizure of power' through his office and his personality.

The structure of the private sector of the economy was similarly unaltered. In 1922 and 1923 the surviving remnants of the wartime planned economy were done away with and the autonomy of the free enterprise economy was restored. In 1919 a unified industrial lobby was created with the founding of the National Association of German Industry (RDI). With this move industry sharpened its cutting-edge *vis-à-vis* the state and the trade unions, even though the older elements of competing industrial groups lived on within the new association. During the inflation year of 1923 and in the period of stabilization that began in 1924 the process of economic concentration continued, achieving a new dimension with the founding of the United Steelworks in 1926, through IG-Farben and the formation of a Banking Group of Four (the D-D banks). In spite of the growing influence of the engineering, electrical and chemical industries, which between 1926 and 1931 provided the RDI with its president in Carl Duisberg of IG-Farben, direction of the Association remained with the large Ruhr corporations of the coal, iron and steel industries. It was a similar story with the successor organization to the Farmers' League, the National Rural League (RLB), which as time went on was increasingly dominated by representatives of the East Elbian landed magnates. Notwithstanding all the differences,[78] not least that over attitudes towards the trade unions, in the Weimar state the post-1878 alliance of the old power elites was renewed via the brawl to carry the customs tariff of 1924–5, albeit under circumstances which gave diminished weight to agriculture in comparison with the prewar period. For the formulation of German economic policy,[79] but also in relation to social policy and public policy in general, this alliance had wide-ranging consequences. Through demonstrable co-operation, even in the forefield of foreign trade policy, e.g. for the trade treaties with Poland and France, via the co-ordination of industrial and agricultural interests, a course was charted whose detailed implementation was left to the civil service. After the war, and partly because of the experience of war, the degree of collaboration between the syndicates and the ministries actually increased in the direction of an economic revisionism, for national recovery seemed possible only through economic and political co-operation. Given the tradition of 'authoritarian capitalism' in Germany, it was natural that such co-operation proceeded much more directly under conservative cabinets than under leftist ones. Its achievements during the war, and particularly the demise of courtly and aristocratic society as the pinnacle of the social pyramid after the end of the princely households, gave the captains of industry, especially the 'Ruhr barons' of whom Hugo Stinnes was typical, an aura and a respect that were unattainable in the *Kaiserreich*, where they had had to work their way up the hierarchy, at heavy financial cost and in competition with the aristocracy, to the post of Commercial Privy Councillor. Under the republic, by contrast, they enjoyed much greater real influence.

The trade unions under Legien's leadership (another element of continuity) held fast to their social reformist course and were not prepared to jeopardize their organization through socialization experiments and by supporting the 'workers' and soldiers' councils'. Their exclusive concern was recognition and consolidation of their place within the prevailing economic system and to extend the position they had won in November 1916 during the war. Through the founding of the 'joint industrial alliance' (ZAG) with the organized employers in the so-called Legien-Stinnes pact[80] in November 1918 they believed it possible to avoid mass unemployment and to raise wages. Yet the ZAG enjoyed the support of only a puny segment of organized business, mainly in the chemical and electrical trade, who planned eventually to drop their alliance with the pre-industrial castes in favour of collaboration with organized labour. The far stronger section of the employers, that grouped around the coal, iron and steel industrialists, regarded the alliance with Legien as a mere temporary expedient designed exclusively to steer the free enterprise system safely through the shoals of socialization. This group, whose spokesmen were Ruhr industrialists like Reusch, Thyssen, Springorum, Vögler and Kirdorf, remained irreconcilable with the

Weimar polity, even when it was governed by bourgeois cabinets, as it was after 1920. They were not only anti-democratic but, in ideological terms, anti-parliamentary as well. At a very early stage they called for a strong state independent of parties and parliament, and from 1930 onwards they demanded a 'leader'. Hence their close collaboration with the German Nationalists (successor party to the Conservatives) and the right wing of the German People's Party (successor party of the National Liberals), in which the industrial lobby, particularly that of the west, formed a kind of 'veto bloc' against a continuation of social policy.[81] These groups also worked towards a pre-parliamentary authoritarian corporate state. This may be seen in the ideas for a reconstitution of the state prevalent in the conservative camp of the 'resistance' to Hitler during the Second World War, for these harked back not to the Weimar republic, to democracy, but to the Bismarckian empire, even to the pre-Bismarckian era. That the Reichstag elections of May 1928 registered a swing to the left, after years of relative prosperity and bourgeois cabinets which included even German Nationalist (DNVP) participation, created alarm among the bourgeois parties and the interest groups of industry and agriculture. In place of the moderate Count Westarp, the Pan-German Hugenberg now became chairman of the German Nationalist People's Party, and Prelate Kaas, on the far right of his party, was elected chairman of the Centre Party.

Right-wing circles were irritated by the return of a Social Democrat to the office of chancellor, even though he headed a 'grand coalition' government in which the DVP reluctantly participated and which the DNVP fought remorselessly. As early as the spring of 1929 the *Deutsche Allgemeine Zeitung* or *DAZ* (close to industry and popular reading among the educated classes) demanded 'a ministry of civil renewal' with power to dissolve the Reichstag and governing through an 'enabling law'. The bourgeois world was to take a stand against that of the proletariat. Such circles had begun to look to Italian fascism no later than 1928. Hans Reupke, a CDI syndic, published a book on Italian fascism which made a particularly favourable impression on Vögler. He published newspaper articles on the same subject in the *Tag*. Here the kernel of fascism was identified as 'national socialism plus anti-Marxism'; it was the authoritarian state minus socialism. (No doubt the emphasis was determined with pedagogic intent and in reference to the national socialism of Hitler's party.) Mussolini was allegedly imbued with the 'overriding importance of the business mentality'; fascism was a 'pathfinder of the capitalist system', destined to 'annihilate and supplant the class concept which permeates the modern world'.

Similar to the May elections of 1928 in its alarming impact on industry was the trade unions' demand for 'codetermination' in the larger enterprises. Although it probably appears today as an over-estimation of the possibilities of the time and of the cohesion of the Weimar system, this demand was raised in 1928 at the Hamburg congress of the Free Trade Unions. This precipitated the employers' struggle against the so-called 'political' wage,[82] which took the form of a lockout of 250,000 workers in the iron and steel industry and lasted for several months, from 1928 into 1929. In the great economic crisis, a capitalist crisis of global dimensions, which in Germany under prevailing conditions became a political crisis, particular employer groups representing 'reform capitalism' demonstrated a willingness to resume co-operation with the trade unions in a revival of the ZAG of 1919–24 (as, for example, the lignite industrialist Silverberg had already indicated in his well-known speech of 1926,[83] albeit with no practical result). However, since the bulk of small business had also taken fright at the Social Democratic demand for 'economic democracy', the moderate groups were unable to carry their concept against the opposition of heavy industry, who for their part, as they had done prior to the First World War, envisaged a solution to the crisis and a possible economic revival exclusively in the suppression and destruction of the trade unions. However, not only economic interests but also the 'inherited social mentalities and forms of behaviour' characteristic of 'authoritarian capitalism' were now brought to bear in a sustained attack on the welfare-state component of the Weimar constitution itself.[84] The demand that the collective bargaining system be relaxed or abolished, that compulsory arbitration of labour disputes in particular (as a last resort, when management and labour were unable to reach agreement) be abandoned, and for abolition of state social-security services (social insurance, unemployment relief) formed the components of this offensive. Its objective could be reached only if pushed through under the momentary duress of the crisis, before a possible recovery supervened to enhance the strength of the trade unions.

Large-scale industry had viewed with growing displeasure the government of the grand coalition, welcomed its fall and at first held high hopes of the Brüning government, whose deflationary policy of drastic cuts in government expenditure and revenue (tax reductions) went a long way towards meeting industry's demands for a 'self-healing' of the economy. In fact, his policy of slashing both wages and prices led to ever greater contraction of the economy and correspondingly rising numbers of unemployed, whose distress the NSDAP sought to exploit.[85] Although Brüning's economic policy significantly deepened the crisis, it did not go anywhere near far enough for the leaders of the business community. They demanded a further round of wage cuts and abstention from price-reduction measures, and when Brüning failed to practise this policy with sufficient vigour they abandoned him to his fate in the autumn of 1931.[86] In view of the weakness of the bourgeois-liberal forces and the vulnerability of the workforce, at war with itself in two hostile parties, the parliamentary-democratic camp now had its back to the wall while, on the other side, the old power elites of landed wealth, industry, army and civil-service mandarins now appeared to champion order and recovery from a position of greater strength than ever. Of these, the numerically small group of landed aristocrats, together with the Reichswehr (Schleicher), effected the overthrow of Chancellor Brüning, although in the midst of his policy of deflation he had put millions at the disposal of both, through rearmament and *Osthilfe* (agricultural subsidies to assist farming in the east). For the President, the agrarians, the army and industry (Hindenburg told Brüning at their last meeting, 'The rule of the trade-union secretaries must cease!'), not the least of the factors necessitating Brüning's dismissal was his inability to carry out the commission he had received from Hindenburg to remove Social Democracy from any share in government once and for all: to the political right, it seemed, on the contrary, that Brüning was dependent on SPD toleration.

From the very beginning, conservative Germany, especially the great estates and big business, welcomed Papen's authoritarian state, aiming at permanently neutering the trade unions and the political labour movement, as the fulfilment of their long-cherished hopes – constitutionally, in economic policy and in the realm of social policy. Actually, this experiment sailed very close to civil war, with its unpredictable consequences, for the army alone was ultimately unable to provide a sufficiently stable base for an authoritarian policy against the left. This dilemma confronting the Papen government was in fact very much in the minds of representatives of the conservative ruling strata, of big business above all, but increasingly oppressive also to Papen himself (as demonstrated by his club speech of September 1932), namely the awareness that it was impossible for them to mobilize mass support for their own interests as a counterweight to industrial labour. Yet this is precisely what was offered them by Hitler, who, with the aid of anti-Semitism and an extreme nationalism, had welded together a mass party, albeit one formed principally from the crisis-victims of uprooted *Mittelstand*,[87] lower middle-class and peasant elements. Before an accommodation could be reached,[88] certain reservations on the conservative side had first to be eliminated. There was no disagreement on rejection of the Weimar democracy, but industry was still sceptical of the vulgar demagogy and, above all, the petty-bourgeois anti-capitalism of the Nazi Party. After 1930 Hitler tried to bridge these differences. Consciously pursuing a double strategy, he sought to make clear in intimate discussions with industry representatives that his assumption of office would mean no significant change in the existing free-enterprise system. At the same time he held fast to his party's customary style of agitation, so as not to jeopardize his influence with the voting masses. This tactic was still in operation in the summer of 1932. While the party fought the Reichstag elections on the so-called Strasser programme, wooing both the lower middle classes and the unemployed with a pointedly anti-cyclical economic policy, Hitler, using the good offices of Schacht, entered into private relations with big business. After the July elections of 1932, on the advice of Schacht and presumably also in response to heavy-industry intervention, Hitler dropped the Strasser programme and then, in autumn 1932, gave the nod to industry by promulgating a new, pro-industry 'economic construction programme' that was to be binding on the whole party. This programme focused primarily on the tax cuts already initiated by Papen. In this way the man with a mass-following at his disposal (still; and this factor had to be exploited!), who had none the less virtually sacrificed the petty-bourgeois and anti-capitalist tendencies within his party, became increasingly attractive to heavy industry as a potential alliance partner. Lower middle-class anti-capitalism was replaced by a big-business production policy which was also the only avenue to the large-scale rearmament objective desired by both industry and Hitler. This process of accommodation received a further boost when in early December Hitler cold-shouldered Strasser – because of his sympathy for the 'trade-union axis' that Schleicher as chancellor had striven to construct as a political prop by promoting the Christian and the socialist trade unions – and Papen simultaneously began making overtures to Hitler. Thus the preconditions for the 'bracketing concept' were created. Both of them, Papen and Hitler, practised an authoritarian style of leadership, Papen and Hugenberg together functioning as guarantors of the economic interests of the bourgeoisie, while Hitler brought to the alliance the mass-base which the others lacked.

It is correct that it was not the electoral results which brought Hitler to power (the November 1932 elections were a setback for the Nazis) but the policy of the power elites, and that in January 1933 an important part in Hitler's appointment as Reich chancellor was played by the Prussian Junkers,[89] a 'pre-industrial' group living, like the President, under the cloud of an *Osthilfe* scandal. On the other hand, it is no less true that important business groups also participated (e.g., through petitions to Hindenburg, and via Papen and Schröder) in the process whereby power was bestowed on Hitler. To be sure, there were still major differences between business and agriculture in January 1933,[90] and these ignited most readily on the extreme tariff demands of agriculture, which threatened to put at risk the entire German commercial-treaty system. Both sides nevertheless agreed that the NSDAP was a political force which must be won over; that a mere return to the 'Papen system' was out of the question; that Nazi participation in government was, in any case, the lesser evil *vis-à-vis* Schleicher's attempt to draw the trade unions into the presidial state and so to preserve certain welfare-state elements in the Weimar political system, for the most influential farming and business groups had been persistently pursuing the abolition of these very elements since 1928. For this reason they had hailed as their own the Papen government which in September 1932 permitted a reduction of up to 50 per cent in contractual wage-rates, even if they were obliged to admit to the unpopularity of 'such a blatant régime of economic and social privilege', and even though their perennial call for the 'strong man' and the 'leader' finally led to Hitler. To adhere to this view is not to presuppose a homogeneity of all interests. Yet it is untenable to speak of this, as was asserted apologetically after 1945, as a question of saving the democratic state by the rational conservatives, as they liked to see themselves, 'taming' the irrational popular tribune through their numerical superiority in the cabinet. Rather did these groups seek to put the NSDAP chairman to work in the service of their social and economic, even their military and power-political interests and objectives. What united both sides, Hitler and the old elites, however much they diverged in motivation and political vocabulary, was their commitment to the national power-state at home and abroad, and it is this which made possible the collaboration between these dissimilar partners. In the organized subordination of the people to the holders of political power, and in bellicose assertiveness and expansion, there was a harking-back to the traditions of Imperial Germany (the day at Potsdam, for example), against which background the Weimar years necessarily appeared as a confused apparition of disorganization and weakness. With the destruction of the parties and trade unions and the creation of a totalitarian state-directed union in the 'German Labour Front', objectives were attained that Bismarck had striven in vain to realize.

Here, however, domestic and foreign policy objectives cannot be separated. Unquestionably, those business magnates who supported National Socialism before 1933 did so 'precisely for the sake of the goals realized immediately following the change of government – elimination of the trade unions and the political labour movement, abolition of the parliamentary system of government, rearmament' – all of which were intended to bring them and their businesses back onto the profit side of the ledger, 'at the cost of a muzzled working class'.[91] Yet with a 'muzzled working class' there was no longer any political force to offer serious resistance to those who would challenge the status quo in Europe and the world, whether by economic means, through the use of military force or even by means of war. In their desire for peace and disarmament, the German workers were just as isolated in the Weimar republic as they had been in Imperial Germany, and this despite the principled support which the SPD and the trade unions had given to the idea of national defence, for example, at the 1929 Magdeburg party congress.[92] Yet it was their very rejection of an excessive rearmament policy and a revisionist and expansionist policy based on coercion that led to their political castration in Prussia, at the hands of the 'reaction' in the form of the Papen cabinet, as early as 20 July 1932.[93]

Economic Interests and Foreign Policy

A line of continuity is also exhibited in German foreign policy after 1919. The meaning of what historians have all too innocently termed 'revisionism' was that the Reich, or the surviving elites controlling the levers of power, refused to recognize the new European order resulting from the war and that, by one means or another, these elites were determined to alter the status quo of 1919. The principal 'revisionist' forces were the Foreign Office, the army, the Commerce Ministry, the parties of the right and the economic and social groups associated with them. Their aim was the restoration of the German Great Power position in Europe and ultimately in the world, a goal also shared by Stresemann. This was not possible by military means in the decade after 1919. Stresemann therefore made deliberate diplomatic and political use of the economic opportunities open to the Reich and of cultural realities like the minorities question, and it was for this purpose that he sought German admission to the League of Nations. But his final objective of transforming the European status quo was incompatible with the intentions of his counterpart Briand, whose goal was the maintenance of the 1919 settlement. Stresemann's refusal to enter into an eastern Locarno pact with Poland and Czechoslovakia reveals the offensive character of his policy. Even if he was unable, without completely discrediting his Locarno policy, to raise the question of an *Anschluss* with Austria,[94] this was nevertheless among his long-term objectives. He publicly proclaimed his aim to achieve a Reich of 70 million Germans in December 1918, and again in January 1925, this time in strict secrecy, he reformulated it for the Reich cabinet as 'the creation of a state whose political frontiers encompass all parts of the German people living within the identifiably German area of Central Europe and desiring incorporation in the Reich'. There would also be within this Central European state, he added, 'members of foreign nationalities living beside our compatriots under German suzerainty'. While Briand sought 'security' for France, Stresemann was working for 'equal rights' as a mere stepping-stone to the restoration, even the enlargement of Germany's old power position. The incompatibility in the French and German positions on the Continent became clear in the German reply to Briand's memorandum on European union, which was conceived as a diplomatic move against a possible Austro-German union, i.e. against German hegemonial ambitions in eastern and south-eastern Europe. For this very reason the Briand proposal was rejected by the Brüning-Curtius government, which believed itself to be combating French hegemony.[95]

The *Anschluss* issue was of power-political importance in that Austria functioned as a German spring-board to south-eastern Europe and beyond into the Near East, as it had done prior to 1914 and during the First World War. Thus from 1925 onwards the foreign policy of the Reich clearly aimed at creating in east-central and south-eastern Europe a string of client states which, with the exception of the claim on Poland (the Polish corridor), were not to be subject to territorial annexations but were to be subjected to thoroughgoing German economic penetration. The Foreign Office regarded a 'customs union' as a particularly 'appropriate means' to this specific end 'as it highlights the economic facts and obscures from outside observation the political ramifications', which were envisaged as conducing to an 'almost unlimited dependence on Germany' (already achieved by 1925 in the case of Lithuania).[96] With the 1931 Brüning-Schober attempt to create an Austro-German customs union – an attempt which had devastating economic as well as diplomatic repercussions – the Foreign Office also entertained hopes of being able to attract Czechoslovakia and Poland through the force of 'economic necessity', especially if the Baltic states (Estonia, Latvia and Lithuania) should also join this 'commercial grouping'. The conclusion of preferential tariff agreements with Rumania and Hungary in 1931, so it was hoped in the Foreign Office and the Reich Ministry for Commerce, could be followed by similar treaties with Yugoslavia and Bulgaria.

The German economy, in collaboration with the German state, was active in the same direction. After the prohibition of *Anschluss*, German buying into Austrian business, which was particularly heavy in the iron and steel industry (Alpine Mining, for example), offered an avenue for re-entry into the Balkans. Efforts to create a *'Mitteleuropa'* had intensified after 1927 in the reconstitution of the 'Central European Economic Association' *(Mitteleuropäischer Wirtschaftstag)*,[97] a direct successor organization of a similar institution that had existed during the *Kaiserreich* but now fell under the dominating influence of autarkic German big business, whose leading lights belonged to it, as did those of large-scale agriculture. The heads of the national government departments (Karl Ritter of the Foreign Office, Karl Posse of the Ministry for Commerce) gave powerful assistance to this economic expansion through their direct co-operation with the Central European Economic Association. Thus Posse, addressing this body on 19 May 1932, underlined the need to expand the German trading area and to 'camouflage our ultimate political aims' in the process.[98]

There were three variations on this theme. Carl Duisberg, the leading man of IG-Farben, recommended German expansion with rather than against France, so that the great financial strength of France might be exploited to the advantage of the chemical interests of both countries. What he had in mind, on 24 March 1931, was a customs association stretching from Bordeaux to Odessa.[99] A leading spokesman of the Rhenish-Westphalian steel industry and general-secretary of the Long-name Association *(Verein zur Wahrung der gemeinsamen wirtschaftlichen Interessen in Rheinland und Westfalen* – Association for the Protection of Common Economic Interests in the Rhineland and

Westphalia), Schlenker, urged a customs union between Germany, Austria, Czechoslovakia, Rumania and Bulgaria, to create, as he said (on 13 February 1931), a market of 100 million people. He gave this programme a strongly anti-Russian accent, directing it against the massive dumping of grain and manufactures practised by Russia, but it was also envisaged as an economic region united against North America, all of which made it identical with the ideas of 1914–18. Half a year later, on 17 June 1931, at a huge Berlin meeting of the Association of German Iron and Steel Industrialists, the same man declared himself still more pointedly in favour of the creation of a great *Mitteleuropa* trading area as a front directed against Communist Russia.[100] From 1933–4 until the eve of the Second World War, the Foreign Office and the Reich Ministry for Commerce pursued these plans uninterruptedly in their efforts to create an extended economic unit *(Grossraumwirtschaft)*, now directed to a so-called 'war economy' *(Wehrwirtschaft)*, one of its forms being bilateral treaties with all the Balkan states and Turkey.[101]

Although German economic interests, in their collaboration with government departments prior to 1933, were still primarily concerned with economic objectives in which political aims were more latent and which cannot be equated simply with military expansion, the power-political and bellicose element is abundantly clear in the case of the two conservative groups which, with Hitler, initiated the campaign against the Young Plan in late 1929, which joined the Harzburg front with him in October 1931 and formed a coalition government with him in January 1933– the DNVP and the *'Stahlhelm'*, which were both closely connected with the Protestant church. In them there lived on, in the tradition of the 'Hakatists', the 1914–18 annexationism and the post-1919 Free Corps struggles, an extreme hatred of Poland, which was regarded as the most dangerous enemy of the Reich. In 1928, for instance, the *Stahlhelm* publicly proclaimed, 'with heart and soul we hate the present state . . . because it affords us no prospect of liberating our enslaved fatherland, of purging the German people of the war-guilt lie, of gaining the living-space we need in the east, of making the German people once again capable of defending itself.' In this document Hitler's aims are already anticipated, namely (1) the abolition of the parliamentary system of government, (2) the rearmament of the German people and the restoration of its self-defence capability, and (3) the conquest of living-space in the east. At the *Stahlhelm* congress in Breslau in 1931 a formal declaration of war was issued against Poland, causing enormous excitement there. Another example would be the party leader Hugenberg explaining in his 1931 public speeches that Germany, a 'fenced-in people' *(Volk ohne Raum)*, a 'people in chains', required for its 'vigorous race' new areas for colonization in the east in addition to a colonial empire in Africa, that Germany needed 'freedom and space' which the German people could acquire only through self-help. A further example was the German Nationalist deputy von Freytagh-Loringhoven, addressing a 1932 conference of his party's leaders, proclaiming the goal of first revising the nation's frontiers, above all in the east, and creating a 'Greater German Empire', and then 'gaining new land, new space for our people' and 'restoring it as a spiritually and physically healthy peasant ethnicity'. Here we have an ideology which is scarcely distinguishable from National Socialist doctrine, right up to the 'blood and soil' theory, and at the same time a sketch of the temporal launching of the action programme, as this was subsequently observed in common with the National Socialist coalition partner.[102]

Beyond the end of the war there survived in these conservative groups an intellectual tradition which saw nationalism and Christianity as being practically identical. As German revisionism began in the late twenties and with growing singlemindedness to pursue aims which could be achieved only by means of war, the attitude of the church to war necessarily gained in importance. In 1930 Otto Dibelius published his book, *Is War Permissible according to the Will of God?* And he answered his question by combining Luther, Hobbes and Social Darwinism:

> In the history of mankind one violent deed follows another, war follows upon war. Destiny is shaped through an endless struggle of all against all. War has always been with us. Everything we call civilisation has been determined by great decisions taken on the battlefield . . . war is a natural rule of life among peoples. Against it, religion makes no protest. Neither does Christianity object.

From this spiritual outlook no resistance was to be expected to a policy which embraced war in realizing its goals.[103] It is therefore understandable that both the Protestant and Catholic churches, the latter from a natural-law standpoint, did not hesitate, when war again became a reality in 1939, once again to urge the faithful to obey the authorities and to look for a divine purpose in all that transpired.

At the universities the historical profession remained bound to a nationalist and conservative tradition in the vast majority of cases. Certainly, the 'republicans only by force of circumstances' *(Vernunftrepublikaner)* like Friedrich Meinecke and Ernst Troeltsch, who adopted a constitutional and social-policy position which was very close to that of the German Democratic Party, remained few and uninfluential. The veneration of a handful of outsiders (like Eckart Kehr, Arthur Rosenberg or Johannes Ziekusch today) should not be allowed to obscure the contours of the then dominant outlook. In the interpretation of Luther and Bismarck, as previously during the war with the jubilees of 1915 and 1917, a philosophically vindicated anti-Western line was consistently apparent. Thus Gerhard Ritter, for example, in his 1925 book on Luther, rejected the 'modern world', as he put it, 'if one chooses to understand by that the spirit of Anglo-Saxon and Romance civilization'. Here one also finds, 'however often a wave of West European thought seems to deluge our spiritual development . . . again and again one notices the German spirit offering resistance to such floods'. From such a source it was not possible to derive a positive relationship with the parliamentary-democratic political system, its toleration being the best one might hope for. Certain it is that the republic could not be defended from this position, even though the 1932 conservative 'strong-state' solution was dearer to the hearts of most of these historians than was the political form arrived at in 1933. The 'Continental power-state' was contrasted with the 'insular welfare state' and, measured against the former, the Weimar republic was judged to be an alien excrescence, something grafted onto German history, unserviceable for the revival of German power. By contrast, the new government of 1933 was perceived as marking the return of the strong state and was therefore viewed from the perspective of the 'day of Potsdam'. Thus, three years later, in his biography of Frederick the Great, Gerhard Ritter depicted a line of continuity in these terms: 'And finally the day of Potsdam, the solemn opening of the "Third Reich", established an externally formal link with the proudest traditions of Old Prussian history'.[104] This was the same spiritual tradition in which the army lived.

The Army and the Power-State Tradition

Beside the elites of agriculture and industry, the Foreign Office and the Commerce Ministry, the universities and the churches, the leading elements of the army through the 1920s and 1930s stood out as the strongest pillars of the traditional social structures and political ambitions of the Wilhelmine Germany of prewar and wartime vintage.

Thanks to the so-called Ebert-Groener pact of 9 November 1918 and the conditions that the army managed to impose on the government of the People's Commissioners in November and December, the army had preserved a degree of independence which left it virtually untouched by political change.[105] It was a 'birth defect' of the republic that it relied upon an officer corps, in the words of F. L. Carsten, 'from which no one could expect that it would welcome or be converted to the new order'. Part of the problem, no doubt, was that the Social Democrats lacked the confidence to build up a republican army. Under Seeckt, whom Ebert appointed to head the army, the social composition of the officer corps was therefore confined to 'a wafer-thin upper stratum' consisting, for the most part, of General Staff officers with a large proportion of aristocrats. Living in the past, and for the future of the 'nation', this army maintained a cool and frequently hostile distance towards the existing state, towards the Weimar republic.[106]

Thus Joachim von Stülpnagel, head of the army section in the Troops Office, i.e. in the General Staff, outlined the Reichswehr dilemma as follows: it was charged with 'protecting the constitution, of a sick system, in other words; and the preparation of a liberation struggle which the system obstructs'. In 1924, during an in-service lecture entitled 'Thoughts on the War of the Future', the same officer contemplated a renewed war with France as imperative to the survival and future development of the Reich, leaving open only the question of 'when and under which preconditions'. In his well-known memorandum for the Foreign Office in 1926,[107] and taking up Groener's idea of 1919, the same Stülpnagel developed a two-stage plan which envisaged that 'in the next stages of her political development Germany [would] aim solely at the recovery of her European position and only much later take up the struggle for recovery of her global position', the latter 'in conflict with the Anglo-American powers'. (In so arguing, he was in accord with the memoranda of Lieutenant General Wandel of the Prussian War Ministry and of Moltke and Ludendorff of the General Staff when in 1911 and 1912 they successfully championed a military priority over the hitherto favoured naval armaments requirements, while nevertheless giving whole-hearted approval to the navy's ultimate function.[108]) Stülpnagel further calculated that what he envisaged as the next step, namely the re-annexation of the economically indispensable lost territories of 1919 and *Anschluss* with Austria, would lead to conflict with France and its allies in East-Central Europe, namely, Poland and Czechoslovakia. What this allegedly boiled down to was 'stripping France of its domineering military power'. The contemplated route to this goal lay via the forum of the disarmament conference, which should also help to promote German rearmament, thereby eliminating the 'anomalous' limitations on German armaments. Planned army and navy manoeuvres in the years 1926 to 1929 covered the contingency of a two-front war with Poland and France.

If, following Seeckt's dismissal, the Reichswehr leaders co-operated more closely with the civilian political leadership, this did not mean that the Reichswehr had moved to the left. On the contrary, this was no more than a tactical ploy to finance and provide political security for the rearmament programmes (illegal, according to the Versailles Treaty) begun by the Luther, Müller and Brüning governments and pushed through with the aid of a committee of three secretaries of state, and in deliberate deception of parliament.[109] The Reichswehr thereby moved not one whit closer to becoming the guarantor of the republic and its democracy. Backed by their party's defence committee, three leading men of the Social Democratic Party (Chancellor Müller, Interior Minister Severing and the Prussian Premier Braun) had indeed succeeded in reducing socialist reservations in regard to the Reichswehr and its rearmament. It is also true that the 1929 Magdeburg SPD party congress established 'guidelines on defence policy and matters of national defence'. But this did not go far enough for a Reichswehr leadership that was unable to reach agreement with the Prussian government on the use of patriotic societies, including the SA and the *Stahlhelm* – both extreme enemies of the republic – for frontier defence, especially since, in the armoured cruisers question, the Social Democrats gave notice of the limits of their co-operativeness.[110] Mistrust of SPD 'pacifism' therefore continued. In the best tradition of Seeckt, the officer corps and the generals consistently remained aloof from the Weimar state, unlike the 'desk generals' who seemed to be too closely associated with this state. In any event, as early as the Müller government (October 1928) the army, like the navy and the air force, was given its first Four-Year Rearmament Plan, for the period 1928 to 1932, which in 1932, under Brüning, was followed by a second such plan, to last until 1938. This development was possible only because there had already been developing since the early 1920s a close relationship between the Reichswehr and the industries concerned with supplying all three branches of the armed forces, through which relationship preconditions were created, at the technical, organizational and financial levels, for the starting-point of the mid and late 1920s.[111]

In the meantime, thanks to the literature of what Wette terms 'soldierly nationalism',[112] diffused through such writings as those of the Jünger brothers, W. Beumelburg, E. von Salomon, Schauwecker, Oswald Spengler and Ludendorff, a militaristic conception of society had come to prevail. It conflicted with the reconciliation tendency of the Stresemann era and further exaggerated that predominance of the military factor in German public affairs which had already been instilled by tradition. Its function was to enhance the chances of victory in the next war. It was the thought of the so-called 'reformers' or 'revolutionaries' which deduced from the World War the theory of 'total war'.[113] This placed economic and propaganda warfare beside and on an equal footing with armed combat. Accordingly, the entire nation was to be earmarked for 'defence duties', and even the political leadership was to be subordinated to this task. For such a purpose, the system of parliamentary democracy appeared inappropriate, and the transition to the strong state, as prosecuted by Schleicher – he overthrew three chancellors – seemed indispensable. Together with German policy at the disarmament conference, which was used from first to last as a vehicle for German rearmament, all this led directly, in terms of military policy, to the Hitler era.

As indicated above, the incidence of the Hitler cabinet in 1933 would not have been possible without the collaboration of the conservative elites (and the concurrence of all the bourgeois parties in the 'enabling law', in which the attitude and motivation of the Centre Party are of particular importance) or without that of the Reichswehr. The Hitler-Blomberg agreement preceding Hitler's clash with the SA, the revolutionary wing of the NSDAP, in June 1934 was again the precondition to Reichswehr acquiescence in a personal oath to Hitler after the death of Hindenburg and thus to the final consolidation of the Führer's position, now also as head of state.[114] This declaration of mutual loyalty found its echo in the two-pillars theory of party and armed forces (henceforth the 'Wehrmacht') as the twin foundations of the new state.[115] The Reichswehr was grateful that the armed forces were freed of all obligation to intervene in the internal arena (the situation prevailing before, during and after the First World War) as this task was now the responsibility of the police, the SA and the SS, while group solidarity and ideological training were now matters for the party. As 'arms bearer of the nation', the Wehrmacht was therefore now in a position to prepare exclusively for its function in an external conflict. The personal oath to the commander in chief and the restoration of what the army regarded as 'the honour of the uniform' (Blomberg's expression at the outbreak of war in 1939) created a bond between the new state and the army which, for the majority of the Wehrmacht, survived until 1945.

On the army's side, this pact of 1933–4 had been entered into in order to uphold the traditional position of the officer corps in the state and society. As they understood it, this embraced at the very least a right to consultation, if not to enjoy the central influence in the political decision-making process. To this extent, the military leaders believed they had merely recovered a position they had occupied during the *Kaiserreich* but had seen neglected under Weimar and in need of remedy. Hence the support given by the army leaders to Hitler's Great-Power policy based on an excessive arms build-up – because they believed their own position secure only in a powerful state governed by authoritarian means, and because the restoration of the German Great-Power position accorded with their own convictions.

During the first years of the Hitler government the army, driven by the energy of the Chief of the General Staff Beck, backed by Foreign Minister von Neurath (both belonging to the conservative elites), and in the closest collaboration with big business, prosecuted the rearmament programme more ruthlessly than Hitler himself (Deist speaks of 'unbounded' rearmament), who was obliged to move with outwardly greater caution, having recourse to speeches on peace. This was a rearmament programme which the army fashioned both qualitatively and quantitatively as an offensive weapon.

The navy leadership under Raeder, for whom the 1935 Anglo-German Naval Agreement, with its 35 per cent settlement, was never more than a transitional solution, prepared for Germany's admission to the 'naval power club' and opted for an anti-British policy at a time when Hitler was still angling for an alliance with Britain and even for its neutrality. Within the navy, the Tirpitz intellectual legacy persisted in unbroken continuity, as when it proposed (as in 1914) the conquest of the French Atlantic coast, of Holland and Denmark (to broaden the navy's operational base), and the vigorous construction of a strong home fleet as well as an overseas fleet of four divisions to operate independently on the high seas. (Referring to such proposals emanating from the navy chief Carl, Deist speaks of unreality, hubris, quixotic fantasy and apocalyptic utopias, for these plans envisaged a struggle with half to two-thirds of the entire globe.[116]) Hitler personally began to push naval rearmament only when disappointed in his expectations of Britain.

In the course of the Four-Year Plan of 1936, the character of this rearmament on land, at sea and in the air produced a shift in the centre of gravity within big business away from the hitherto dominant coal, iron and steel group to the more recent chemical

(IG-Farben) and electrical group[117] – a transition which began in 1932 and continued beyond 1945. However this may be judged by economic and social historians, in the present context the important consideration is that such a growth in power would have been unthinkable without big business, notwithstanding the material and personnel limitations which soon became apparent. In 1939 the bulk of the German populace, despite the most intensive propaganda bombardment to which it was subject, remained unimpressed by talk of menace and 'encirclement'. The plain fact is that there existed no enthusiasm for war, as there had been in 1914. The miseries of war were still too fresh a memory for the masses. Only after the rapid military successes in Poland and France was there a brief and temporary change in mood.

Vis-à-vis the First World War, there was no qualitative leap entailed in the military contest with Poland and France in 1939 and 1940. This was similarly planned to take the form of localized lightning wars *(Blitzkriege)* and lay well with the logic, or at least the risk factor, of revisionist policy. Even the 1941 campaign against Russia was planned and initiated as a *Blitzkrieg*. In this campaign, incidentally, as Hillgruber maintains, the army leaders found themselves in unison with Hitler to a degree unknown in previous campaigns. According to the latest research of the same author, the to this extent surprising successes in the French campaign of 1940 encouraged the armed forces command, and especially that of the army, to believe in the possibility of inflicting a decisive defeat on Russia within four to six weeks. The same author sees the source of this 'frivolous' optimism in the Prusso-German General Staff tradition, going back to Moltke and Schlieffen, of the primacy of operational thought, which discouraged 'enemy assessment' (realistic evaluation of the opposing forces and potentialities) and the related estimation of probable logistic or supply problems.[118] Indeed, it is necessary to go further and say that this tradition neglected the issue of the long-term resources of both sides, as was then again demonstrated in the same year with the decision to declare war on America. Only the collapse of the campaign in front of Moscow led to a revival of the theories of 'total war', as crystallized out of the experience of four years of war from the battle of the Marne in November 1914 to November 1918. This revival, together with the 'armament in depth' achieved under Albert Speer,[119] alone made it possible for Germany to wage war for a further three-and-a-half years.

It is noteworthy that the 'campaign' (this expression is itself a continuity, for the First World War was initially so described by the responsible actors) begun in June 1941 as a war of aggression – it was, in reality, a war of conquest – was converted in the retrospection of the participants (Halder, for example), in 1945 and subsequently, into a war for the defence of the Occident.

While the notion of race-war was but an exaggerated form of the pre-First World War propaganda slogan of the impending showdown between Slav and Teuton, a qualitative difference from the First World War is here apparent in the ideology of anti-Bolshevism (enabling the churches to sanction even this war), the hypertrophy of the 'living-space' idea, the treatment of the population in occupied territories as helots,[120] and plans for the resettlement of 30 million people *(Generalplan Ost)*.

Quite within the bounds of traditional power-politics, on the other hand, was the exploitation of Continental western Europe and, to an even greater extent, of eastern Europe. This was done in the name of the German war effort but equally within the larger framework of an extended economic unit designed both to complete the German national economy and to provide a counter-weight to American economic might.[121]

A further continuity to the pre-First World War era was the hope of 1933 to 1939 that Britain might be kept out of the anticipated Continental war or at least persuaded, by means of peace offers, to abandon the war in the wake of the projected German victories. Britain, in other words, was to be induced to recognize the altered position of the Reich in Europe, especially in eastern Europe, and possibly compelled to agree also to a repartition of overseas possessions and markets, which expectations ran aground on Britain's determination to win through. A similar continuity is apparent in the expectation, such as had existed from 1917 onwards, that Britain could be disabled by an unlimited U-boat war without the US intervening even indirectly. When Japan attacked Pearl Harbor, however, Germany declared war on the USA, thereby provoking direct US intervention against herself. This step was prompted not by a subconscious urge to self-destruction on the part of Hitler; it was rooted in a renewed underestimation of America. As in 1918, the weight of US economic power, which was not to be counterbalanced by any European war economy, and soon that of America's military power as well (based on the most modern military technology), together with the protracted and costly resistance of the Soviet Union, finally also decided the Second World War against Germany.

Conclusion

Neither the 'Third Reich' nor the related Second World War would have been possible without the alliance between the former petty-bourgeois Hitler, the rabble-rouser and monomaniac, and the traditional agrarian and industrial power elites who dominated both the armed forces and the diplomatic service. They 'represented the continuity of the national-state legacy' to a particularly high degree: 'They had consciously experienced the rise of Germany prior to 1914, and they were contemporaneous with the economic and military springs of German Great-Power policy in all its variations. Such massive armaments and gearing of the economy to military preparedness would not have been possible without them.' Over and above mere revision of Versailles, their general objective was the rehabilitation of the German Great-Power position, above all with 'regard to eastern Europe, to an eastern imperium guaranteeing a self-sufficient war economy'. 'In such a political context the use of military force was taken for granted.'[122] This objective had originated during the *Kaiserreich*, led to the First World War, seemed to find realization in the peace of Brest-Litovsk, lay dormant during the interregnum of the Weimar republic (which continued to call itself the German Empire) and gathered momentum during the Third Reich and into the Second World War.

The pertinence of the First World War for the continuity problem in German history is that the 'Third Reich', together with its most significant consequence for world history, the Second World War, must be understood primarily as a reaction to the First World War, as a refusal on the part of the optimates of the German Empire to accept the outcome of the First World War. The 'continuity of error' or of 'illusions' may thus be summed up in two large complexes, each operating in turn with particular force on either the domestic arena or the external environment. On two occasions, during the *Kaiserreich* and in Hitler's Reich, the dominant elites of the German Empire misunderstood the historical and political realities confronting Germany in the modern world. They failed to recognize (1) that their attempt to evade societal change in the age of industry by asserting their privileged social position at home, and by also resorting in an emergency to military expansion abroad, was doomed to failure. They failed to understand (2) that neither their European neighbours nor the USA would ever willingly accept a German hegemony based on military expansion.

Out of the manifold interaction of these two complexes emerged two catastrophic world wars. For the catastrophies of German history were not 1918 and 1945, as German tradition prefers to believe, but rather 1914 and 1933/39, as the Salzburg historian Fritz Fellner reminds us.

To recapitulate: it cannot be emphasized too often or too strongly that continuity is not to be equated with sameness, and least of all is it synonymous with unbroken homogeneity. Unquestionably, there were numerous differences in the scale of the aims, in methods and mentality between Imperial Germany and National Socialist Germany. Above all, Imperial Germany was, even in the exceptional circumstances of the First World War state of siege, a constitutional state *(Rechtsstaat)* with historic roots in liberalism. Hitler's Germany had ceased to be a *Rechtsstaat*: witness the violent removal and outlawing of political opponents; witness the forced resettlement and genocide of Poles and Jews. But however singular the criminal and inhuman features of the Hitler dictatorship may have been, it would be an inadmissible truncation of historical reality to contemplate the 'Third Reich' exclusively from such a vantage-point. What is no less necessary is analysis of the on-going structures and enduring aims of the Prusso-German Empire born in 1866–71 and destroyed in 1945, together with clear identification of the continuous elements within the change and diversity of this Empire and their impact on the international system.

The analysis of these relationships is a major historical challenge which cannot be adequately met by means of Hitler biographies, however high in quality these may be. It is, at the same time, a contribution to the task of strengthening our self-consciousness and the viability of our state. Although a separate development of eighty years' duration cannot be overcome at a single stroke, in the Federal Republic German political life has, by and large, found its way back to the federative, liberal and democratic traditions that were suppressed in the middle of the last century; it has thus arrived at a relaxed and normalized relationship with the outside world in the sense of a peaceful co-operation with all its neighbours, one that is based squarely on existing rather than imagined realities.

Notes

1 G. A. Rein, 'Zum Problem der historischen Kontinuität', *Jahrbuch der Rankegesellschaft* (1955), p. 14 ff.; A. Gerschenkron, 'On the concept of continuity in history', in *Continuity in History and Other Essays* (Cambridge, Mass., 1968); A. Lüdtke, 'Zur Kontinuitätsfrage. Schwierigkeiten mit Konzeption und Methode', *Das Argument*, No. 14 (1972), p. 105 ff.

2 L. Dehio, 'Preussisch-deutsche Geschichte 1640–1945. Dauer im Wechsel', Supplement to *Das Parlament*, 3/61 (18.1. 1961), p. 25 ff.; A. Hillgruber, *Deutschlands Rolle in der Vorgeschichte der beiden Weltkriege* (Göttingen, 1967); idem, *Kontinuität und Diskontinuität in der deutschen Aussenpolitik von Bismarck bis Hitler* (Düsseldorf, 1969); F. Fischer (taking issue with Hillgruber's approach), 'Zum Problem der Kontinuität in der deutschen Geschichte von Bismarck zu Hitler' (lecture delivered at the University of Poznan in October 1971), *Studia Historica Slavo-Germanica*, Vol. 1 (Poznan, 1972), reprinted in Fischer, *Der Erste Weltkrieg und das deutsche Geschichtsbild* (Düsseldorf, 1977), pp. 350–63; J. C. G. Röhl (ed.), *From Bismarck to Hitler. The Problem of Continuity in German History* (London, 1970) (especially F. Fischer, 'A Comparison of German Aims in the Two World Wars'); K. Hildebrand, 'Hitlers Ort in der Geschichte des Preussisch-deutschen Nationalstaates', *Historische Zeitschrift*, vol. 217 (1973), pp. 548–632; A. Hillgruber, *Grossmachtpolitik und Militarismus im 20. Jahrhundert. Drei Beiträge zum Kontinuitätsproblem* (Düsseldorf, 1974); T. Nipperdey, '1933 und Kontinuität der deutschen Geschichte', *Historische Zeitschrift*, vol. 227 (1978), pp. 86–111.

3 How deeply the German historical and political consciousness was transformed after 1866 is revealed in the book by the liberal historian Hermann Baumgarten, *Der Liberalismus. Eine Selbstkritik* (Berlin, 1866), and in the programmatic statement of the Berlin Hegelian Adolf Lasson (written under the impression of the battle of Königgrätz), *Das Culturideal und der Krieg* (Berlin, 1868), in which he depicted war, rather than peace, as the natural condition among states.

4 K. A. von Müller, 'An Preussen!' in 'Nationale Kundgebung deutscher und österreichischer Historiker', special issue of the *Süddeutsche Monatshefte*, Munich, September 1914, p. 826 ff.

5 Letter from Bethmann Hollweg to the Crown Prince (November 1913), rejecting a memorandum by Konstantin Baron von Gebsattel (demanding a *coup d'état*), in which Bethmann gave examples of wars fought for the sake of the nation's 'vital tasks' (H. Pogge von Strandmann and I. Geiss, *Die Erforderlichkeit des Unmöglichen* (Frankfurt, 1965), p. 22). A year earlier, in December 1912, during a conversation between Bethmann Hollweg and Colmar von der Goltz on the latter's memorandum dealing with Germany's

position following the First Balkan War, when Goltz called for preventive war: 'The Imperial chancellor's suggestive objection, "But in 1875 Bismarck himself renounced a preventive war", was countered by Goltz (since 1911 a Field Marshal) with the retort, "Correct. Having blessed the fatherland with three preventive wars, he was in a position to do so."' (B. F.Schulte, *Die deutsche Armee 1900–1914* (Düsseldorf, 1977), p. xxvi.)

6 Thus the *Militärwochenblatt* in 1899: 'Both the bourgeois and the aristocratic officer stand for the same principle – the aristocratic as against the democratic outlook' (E. Sagarra, *A Social History of Germany 1648–1914* (London, 1977), p. 241). Compare E. Kehr, 'Das Institut des Königlichen Preussischen Reserveoffiziers', in H.-U. Wehler (ed.) *Das Primat der Innenpolitik* (Berlin, 1965).

7 Thus Martin Kähler in 1872: 'Why is discipline so strong and safe in the Prussian army? For the simple reason that young people, from childhood on, are trained to obedience, to respect for authority in general and to performance of duty', cited in F. Fischer, 'Der deutsche Protestantismus und die Politik im 19. Jahrhundert' (lecture delivered at the Twentieth Congress of German Historians in September 1949), *Historische Zeitschrift*, vol. 171 (1951), p. 497.

8 Among the German people, so the former Prussian Minister for Commerce and promoter of social policy von Berlepsch lamented in 1904, it was still more widely believed than in any other industrialized nation 'that the strike was a revolutionary movement directed against the natural right of the master who pays the wage, that the man in receipt of a wage should be grateful that the existence of himself and his family was secured through the provision of work, that it was frivolous to use a favourable opportunity to press for, or attempt to gain by coercion, an increase in wages or a reduction in working hours, that only greed and the revolutionary current of the age were instilling in workers the desire to organize in free associations', cited in K. Saul, 'Staatsintervention und Arbeitskampf im wilhelminischen Reich, 1904–1914', *Sozialgeschichte heute. Festschrift zum 70. Geburtstag von Hans Rosenberg* (Göttingen, 1974), p. 481.

9 H. Böhme, 'Politik und Ökonomie in der Reichsgründungs- und späten Bismarckzeit', in M. Stürmer (ed.) *Das kaiserliche Deutschland. Politik und Gesellschaft 1870 bis 1918* (Düsseldorf, 1970), pp. 26 ff., 40 f., 48; idem, *Deutschlands Weg zur Grossmacht* (Cologne, 1966), p. 530 ff.

10 H.-P. Ullmann, *Der Bund der Industriellen. Organisation, Einfluss und Politik klein- und mittelbetrieblicher Industrieller im Deutschen Kaiserreich 1895–1914* (Göttinger, 1976).

11 S. Mielke, *Der Hansa-Bund für Gewerbe, Handel und Industrie 1909–1914. Der gescheiterte Versuch einer antifeudalen Sammlungspolitik* (Göttingen, 1976).

12 G. Schmidt, 'Parlamentarisierung oder "Präventive Konterrevolution"? Die deutsche Innenpolitik im Spannungsfeld von Sammlungsbewegungen und latenter Reformbestrebungen 1907–1914', in G. A. Ritter (ed.) *Gesellschaft, Parlament und Regierung* (Düsseldorf, 1974), p. 276 f.

13   K. Epstein, *Matthias Erzberger und das Dilemma der deutschen Demok-ratie* (Berlin and Frankfurt, 1962), p. 113. Accordingly, the Centre did not, as Schmidt maintains (see note 12), 'escape the anti-socialist agitation conducted in the service of the *status quo* interests of the right-wing ruling cartel'.

14   K. Saul, *Staat, Industrie, Arbeiterbewegung im Kaiserreich. Zur Innen-und Aussenpolitik des Wilhelminischen Deutschland 1903–1914* (Düssel-dorf, 1974).

15   P. Winzen, *Bülows Weltmachtkonzept. Untersuchungen zur Frühphase seiner Aussenpolitik 1897–1901* (Boppard, 1977), pp. 25, 27–36.

16   V. R. Berghahn, *Der Tirpitz-Plan. Genesis und Verfall einer innenpolitis-chen Krisenstrategie unter Wilhelm II.* (Düsseldorf, 1971). Compare F. Fischer, 'Recent works on German naval policy', *European Studies Review*, vol. 5, no. 4 (1975), p. 443 ff.

17   Baroness Spitzemberg, diary entry of 14.3.1903, *Das Tagebuch der Baronin Spitzemberg. Aufzeichnungen aus der Hofgesellschaft des Hohenzollern-reiches*, ed. Rudolf Vierhaus (Göttingen, 1960), p. 428; dtv edn, p. 210.

18   E. Kehr, *Schlachtflottenbau und Parteipolitik 1894–1901* (Berlin, 1930).

19   See P. M. Kennedy, *The Rise and Fall of British Naval Mastery* (London, 1976), p. 205 ff., especially 'The German naval challenge'.

20   H. Plehn (Berlin, 1913), p. 1, cited in F. Fischer, *Krieg der Illusionen. Die deutsche Politik 1911–1914* (Düsseldorf, 1969), p. 458 (hereafter cited as *Krieg*).

21   '*Mittelafrika*' in the 'September Programme' (9.9.1914), in F. Fischer, *Griff nach der Weltmacht. Die Kriegsziele des kaiserlichen Deutschland 1914–1918*, 4th edn (Düsseldorf, 1971), p. 118 (hereafter cited as *Griff*). See also Solf references in *Griff*, pp. 115 ff., 414.

22   See P. C. Witt, *Die Finanzpolitik des deutschen Reiches 1903 bis 1913* (Lübeck and Hamburg, 1970); idem, 'Reichsfinanzen und Rüstungspolitik 1898–1914', in *Marine und Marinepolitik 1871–1914* (Düsseldorf, 1972), pp. 146–77.

23   Schulte, *Die deutsche Armee*, pp. 263–4.

24   Schulte, *Die deutsche Armee*, p. 264. See also B. Prince von Bülow, *Denkwürdigkeiten*, Vol. 2 (Berlin, 1930), p. 198.

25   *Krieg*, p. 105 f., 106 f.

26   *Krieg*, p. 131.

27   See J. C. G. Röhl, 'An der Schwelle zum Weltkrieg. Eine Dokumentation über den "Kriegsrat" vom 8.12.1912', *Militärgeschichtliche Mitteilungen*, vol. 26, no. 1 (1977), pp. 77–134; idem, 'Die Generalprobe. Zur Geschichte und Bedeutung des "Kriegsrates" vom 8.12.1912', in D. Stegmann, B.-J. Wendt and P. C. Witt (eds), *Industrielle Gesellschaft und politisches System* (Bonn, 1978), pp. 357–73. Compare A. Gasser, 'Der deutsche Hegemonialkrieg von 1914', in I. Geiss and B.-J. Wendt (eds), *Deutschland in der Weltpolitik des 19. und 20. Jahrhunderts* (Düsseldorf, 1973), pp. 307–40.

28   Schulte, *Die deutsche Armee*, pp. 54–93, 314–32; D. Groh, 'Die geheimen

Sitzungen des Reichshaushaltskommission am 24.–25.4.1913', *Internationale Wissenschaftliche Korrespondenz zur Geschichte der deutschen Arbeiterbewegung*, vol. 7, nos. 11–12 (1971), p. 29 ff.

29 M. Freund, '1914 ist nicht 1939', *Die Politische Meinung*, vol. 9, no. 97 (1964), p. 60; idem, 'Bethmann Hollweg, der Hitler des Jahres 1914?' in E. W. Count Lynar (ed.), *Deutsche Kriegsziele 1914–1918* (Frankfurt, 1964), pp. 175–82. For the view of 1939 as a desperate gamble to escape from a situation of economic crisis, see T. W. Mason, *Arbeiterklasse und Volksgemeinschaft* (Opladen, 1975), p. 166.

30 Z. S. Steiner, *The Foreign Office and Foreign Policy 1898–1914* (Oxford, 1969), p. 212.

31 See A. Hillgruber, 'Riezlers Theorie des kalkulierten Risikos und Bethmann Hollwegs politische Konzeption in der Julikrise 1914', *Historische Zeitschrift*, vol. 202 (1966), pp. 333–51.

32 Bethmann Hollweg to Berchtold, 10.2.1913, in *Krieg*, p. 290 f.

33 F. Fellner, 'Die "Mission Hoyos"', in W. Alff (ed.) *Deutschlands Sonderung von Europa* (Frankfurt, Bern and New York, 1984), p. 283 ff.

34 I. Geiss (ed.) *Julikrise und Kriegsausbruch 1914* (Hanover, 1963), Part I, doc. no. 75, pp. 150–2; see also *Griff*, p. 64.

35 *Krieg*, p. 724.

36 On 10.2.1913 Bethmann Hollweg wrote to Berchtold of 'signs indicating that the policy of ententes has passed its zenith and that we may look forward to a reorientation of British policy' (*Krieg*, p. 290 f.). For 1909, see *Krieg*, p. 109 ff.; for 1912, see p. 169 ff.; for 1913, p. 294 ff. On 4.4.1913 Tschirschky wrote to Bethmann Hollweg that if Vienna intended to solve the Balkan question by violent means it was 'all the more vital that matters be so arranged that Russia was put in the wrong and either she or her satellites appeared as the aggressor. Only through a policy which kept this goal in view could one make it possible for Britain to remain neutral, at least initially.' On 29.7.1914 Bethmann Hollweg expressed the view that 'we must await this development [Russian general mobilization – FF] because we should otherwise fail to carry public opinion with us either in Germany or in Britain' (*Krieg*, p. 711).

37 K. Hildebrand, 'Imperialismus, Wettrüsten und Kriegsausbruch 1914', *Neue Politische Literatur*, vol. 20, nos. 2/3 (1975), pp. 112, 341. Hildebrand speaks of 'polycratic chaos', as does W. Mommsen, 'Die latente Krise des wilhelminischen Reiches 1909–1914', in L. Just (ed.), *Handbuch der deutschen Geschichte*, vol. 4, part 1 (Frankfurt, 1973), and, in the same work (p. 94 ff.), Mommsen, 'Die Flucht nach vorn. Julikrise und Kriegsausbruch 1914'. Idem, 'Die latente Krise des wilhelminischen Reiches. Staat und Gesellschaft in Deutschland 1890–1914', *Militärgeschichtliche Mitteilungen*, vol. 23, no. 1 (1974), p. 10. Similarly, H.-U. Wehler speaks of the 'jurisdictional chaos of the Wilhelmine polycracy', of the 'fissured political constitution of the *Kaiserreich*' (also in respect of the war council of 8 December 1912), of the 'growing torpor' caused by 'contending centres of power', by a 'polycracy of competing power centres' (*Das*

Deutsche Kaiserreich 1871–1918 (Göttingen, 1973), pp. 69, 71). See also Schulte, *Die deutsche Armee*, p. xxvi.

38 Report by Nitti, Italian Commerce Minister, on the visit of a delegation of German industrialists in 1913: 'They spoke unashamedly of the need to get their hands on the iron-ore basin of French Lorraine; war appeared to them as a business proposition' (*Krieg*, pp. 340 and 475). And during the war: 'Our [ore] requirements from Germany are secured for sixty years at the most; with Briey, for a further forty years. France has enough ore for 600 years. For the acquisition of Briey we would wage war for another ten years.' (*Krieg*, p. 475). On the *'pénétration pacifique'* and *'la campagne contre l'invasion germanique'*, see *Krieg*, pp. 462 ff., 471 ff.

39 *Krieg*, p. 321.

40 *Krieg*, p. 643 f.

41 Belgium did not behave passively, Italy remained neutral, Rumania did likewise; Turkey concluded an alliance, but did not at once become active militarily; Sweden did not intervene, nor did Greece and Bulgaria; revolts in Poland, the Ukraine and St Petersburg also failed to materialize, as did those expected in India and the Near East.

42 *Basler Nachrichten*, 9 September 1914, No. 426, p. 1; reprinted in F. Fischer, *Der Erste Weltkrieg und das deutsche Geschichtsbild*, p. 7.

43 Riezler diary entry of 1.8.1916, in K. Riezler, *Tagebücher, Aufsätze, Dokumente*, ed. K. D. Erdmann (Göttingen, 1972), p. 368.

44 W. Groener, situation report, lecture delivered at Supreme Headquarters on 19.5.1919, West German Federal Archives, MA, N 42/12, cited in *Krieg*, p. 1 (epigraph).

45 Referring to 'the difficulty which the German experiences in growing accustomed to the mask of world domination that he *must* wear after victory [emphasis in original]. How heavily our centuries-old congenital modesty weighs upon us!' (diary entry of 21.8.1914, in Riezler, *Tagebücher*, p. 200).

46 See Brockdorff-Rantzau's memorandum of 6.12.1915, cited in *Griff*, p. 174.

47 See G. Förster, H. Helmert, H. Otto and H. Schnitter, *Der preussisch-deutsche Generalstab 1640–1965* (East Berlin, 1966), pp. 115, 117; H. Otto, *Schlieffen und der Generalstab* (East Berlin, 1966). See also Schulte, *Die deutsche Armee*, pp. 148–61 on German offensive doctrine; p. 308 ff., on the army and the short or lightning war.

48 Prince Bülow, *Denkwürdigkeiten*, ed. F. von Stockhammern, Vol. 3 (Stuttgart, 1930), p. 148, cit. in *Griff*, 3rd and 4th edns, p. 108.

49 *Griff*, 1st and 2nd edns, p. 110 ff.; 3rd and 4th edns, p. 116 ff.; pocket edn (1977), p. 93 ff.

50 On *'Mitteleuropa'*, see *Griff*, 3rd and 4th editions, pp. 118, 309, n. 11, 310 ff., 315. See also *Krieg*, pp. 765 ff., 771; W. Gutsche, (after numerous publications on the economic interest groups) *Aufstieg und Fall eines kaiserlichen Reichskanzlers. Theobald von Bethmann Hollweg 1856–1921* (Berlin, 1973), especially p. 148 ff.

51 See Gutsche, *Aufstieg und Fall*, p. 141 f.; *Griff*, pp. 156 ff. (on the Ukraine), 158 ff. (on Poland), 164 ff. (on Finland); *Krieg*, p. 753 ff. See also Bethmann Hollweg's conversation with Theodor Schiemann on 16.8.1914, *Krieg*, p. 759.

52 J. Haller, 'Gedanken eines Balten', in 'Nationale Kundgebung deutscher und österreichischer Historiker', *Süddeutsche Monatshefte* 11 (September 1914), p. 815. See also B. Mann, *Die baltischen Länder in der deutschen Kriegszielpublizistik 1914 bis 1918* (Tübingen, 1965).

53 For example, Bethmann Hollweg to Wilhelm II on 11.8.1915, 'If the development of military events and of affairs within Russia itself should facilitate a rollback of the Muscovite empire towards the east and the severance of its western provinces, our emancipation from this incubus in the east would certainly present us with a goal worth striving for' (*Griff*, p. 238). In his Reichstag speech of 19.8.1914 the 'liberation' of the Poles, of Lithuania and Courland from the Russian yoke was proclaimed by Bethmann Hollweg for the first time (*Griff*, p. 238 f.). For the inception of the policy of 'local autonomy' in 1917, see *Griff*, p. 485 ff. The same subject was dealt with in his Reichstag speech of 5.4.1916 in regard to the eastern peoples and the Flemings (*Griff*, p. 291).

54 'Ein Bethmann Hollweg'scher Plan zur Aufteilung Russlands', in two parts, *Alldeutsche Blätter*, No. 16 (17.4.1915) and No. 17 (24.4.1915), referring *inter alia* to 'a seperate Ukrainian state'.

55 *Griff*, p. 650.

56 Conversation with Bülow on 8.8.1914: 'A German-Anglo-French grouping would really be the best guarantee against the dangers threatening European civilization from the barbaric Russian colossus . . . A foreign policy cultural bloc embracing Britain, Germany and France' (*Krieg*, p. 758, citing Bülow, *Denkwürdigkeiten*, Vol. 3, p. 148).

57 *Krieg*, p. 759, citing Bethmann Hollweg's conversation with Tirpitz on 19.8.1914. According to Tirpitz, the Bethmann 'system pointed our policy in the wrong direction by aiming at the destruction of Russia and sparing Britain' (A. von Tirpitz, *Erinnerungen* (Stuttgart, 1920), p. 254).

58 *Griff*, p. 204, memorandum of November 1914 (see W. Boelcke (ed.) *Krupp und die Hohenzollern* (Berlin, 1956), p. 149 f.). Krupp urged military control of Belgium and naval mastery of the nothern coast of France.

59 Bethmann Hollweg, in conversation with Tirpitz on 5.9.1914 (Admiral H. von Pohl, *Aus Aufzeichnungen und Briefen während der Kriegszeit* (Berlin, 1920), p . 46 ff.).

60 This crucial sentence in Tirpitz's letter to Vice Admiral Lans of 30.8.1914 was omitted from the version published in A. von Tirpitz, *Politische Dokumente*, Vol. 2 (Stuttgart and Berlin, 1926), pp. 81–3. The editor of the documents was obviously fully aware of the importance of this sentence. (Its text was kindly drawn to my attention by P. M. Kennedy.)

61 *Krieg*, p. 778, citing M. Erzberger, *Erlebnisse im Weltkrieg* (Stuttgart, 1920), p. 314. See also G. Ritter, *The Sword and the Scepter*, Vol. 3 (Coral Gables, 1972), pp. 38 and 48. On 19.11.1914, acting on information

provided by Falkenhayn on 18.11.1914, Bethmann Hollweg wrote to Under Secretary of State Zimmermann that 'our losses in officers especially are enormous and in many instances irreplaceable' (*Krieg*, p. 778).

62 *Griff*, p. 178 ff.; K. Schwabe, *Wissenschaft und Kriegsmoral. Die deutschen Hochschullehrer und die politischen Grundfragen des Ersten Weltkriegs* (Göttingen, 1969), pp. 21 ff., 22 ('proclamation of 93').

63 *Griff*, p. 190 ff. For the submission of the six business associations (CdI, BdI, BdL, Deutscher Bauernbund, Reichsdeutscher Mittelstandsverband, Christliche Bauernvereine), see p. 194 f. On 'industry and agriculture', see F. Fischer, *World Power or Decline. The Controversy over 'Germany's Army in the First World War'* (London, 1974), p. 85 ff.

64 On Moltke's view of the Slavic peoples, see *Krieg*, p. 782. On Dorpat University (first rector, Karl Dehio; first curator, Theodor Schiemann; inauguration, 15 September 1918), see *Griff*, p. 813 ff. On the question of Germanizing Courland, Livonia and Estonia, see *Griff*, p. 600 ff. On the planned conventions and personal union, see *Griff*, p. 804 ff.

65 As Bethmann Hollweg informed the Central Committee of the Reichstag at the beginning of October in 1916: 'Since the start of the war we have not escaped the error of underestimating the strength of our enemies. We inherited this mistake from peace-time. In the last twenty years our people had developed so amazingly that whole classes succumbed to the temptation of overestimating our undeniably immense resources in relation to those of the rest of the world.' (*Griff*, p. 861).

66 E. Ludendorff (ed.), *Urkunden der Obersten Heeresleitung über ihre Tätigkeit 1916–1918*, (Berlin, 1920), pp. 318–25. See also W. Gutsche (ed.), *Deutschland im Ersten Weltkrieg*, Vol. 2 (January 1915 to October 1917), (Berlin, 1968), p. 555 ff.

67 Bethmann Hollweg to Zimmermann, 19.11.1914, in *Griff*, p. 218.

68 See J. Kocka, *Facing Total War* (Leamington Spa, 1984); F. Zunkel, *Industrie und Staatssozialismus. Der Kampf um die Wirtschaftsordnung in Deutschland 1914–1918* (Düsseldorf, 1974).

69 *Die Arbeiterschaft im neuen Deutschland* (Leipzig, S. Hirzel, 1915). See the foreword of 14.8.1915. On the 'new orientation', see *Griff*, p. 424 ff. (Bethmann Hollweg and Social Democracy), and Gutsche, *Deutschland im Ersten Weltkrieg*, Vol. 2, pp. 223 ff., 259 ff.

70 See G. D. Feldman, *Army, Industry, and Labor in Germany 1914–1918* (Princeton, NJ, 1966), and Gutsche, *Deutschland im Ersten Weltkrieg*, Vol. 2, p. 457 ff.

71 See P. Borowsky, *Deutsche Ukrainepolitik 1918 unter besonderer Berücksichtigung der Wirtschaftsfragen* (Lübeck and Hamburg, 1970); W. Baumgart, *Deutsche Ostpolitik 1918* (Munich, 1966); W. Basler, *Deutsche Annexionspolitik im Polen und im Baltikum 1914–1918* (Berlin, 1962); W. D. Bihl, *Die Kaukasuspolitik der Mittelmächte*, Part I: *Ihre Basis in der Orientpolitik und ihre Aktionen* (Vienna, Cologne and Graz, 1975).

72 J. Petzold (ed.), *Deutschland im Ersten Weltkrieg*, Vol. 3 (November 1917

to November 1918) (Berlin, 1969), p. 268 ff. For Stresemann, see p. 268; von Heydebrand, p. 227 f.; Dibelius, p. 227; 'Central Office', etc., p. 271.

73 G. Mehnert, *Evangelische Kirche und Politik 1917–1919. Die politischen Strömungen im deutschen Protestantismus von der Julikrise 1917 bis zum Herbst 1919* (Düsseldorf, 1959); W. Pressel, *Die evangelische Kriegspredigt im Ersten Weltkrieg 1914–1918* (Göttingen, 1968); K. Hammer, *Deutsche Kriegstheologie 1870–1918. Dokumente*, dtv Wissenschaftliche Reihe 4151 (Munich, 1974).

74 Cited in D. Stegmann, 'Zwischen Repression und Manipulation. Konservative Machteliten und Arbeiter- und Angestelltenbewegung 1910 bis 1918', *Archiv für Sozialgeschichte*, Vol. 12 (1972), p. 401, n. 223.

75 F. L. Carsten, *The Reichswehr and Politics 1918–1933* (Oxford, 1966), pp. 8–9.

76 From the reports and diaries of Albert Hopmann, Sevastopol 1918, 'Vor 50 Jahren – Oktober 1918: Eine Dokumentation', ed. W. Baumgart, Supplement to *Das Parlament*, B 43/68 (26.10.1968), p. 37 f.

77 In the case of the higher civil service this has been demonstrated by Wilhelm Elben in his book, *Das Problem der Kontinuität in der deutschen Revolution 1918–1919. Die Politik der Staatssekretäre und der militärischen Führung vom November 1918 bis Februar 1919* (Düsseldorf, 1965) (Uni. of Hamburg diss. 1959). On the army, the Foreign Office and the bureaucracy, see H. Mögenburg, *Die Haltung der britischen Regierung zur deutschen Revolution 1918–1919* (Uni. of Hamburg diss. 1975), especially chapter 9, '"Change of Heart" oder ideologische Kontinuität?' p. 287 ff.

78 See J. Flemming, 'Zwischen Industrie und christlich-nationaler Arbeiterschaft. Alternativen landwirtschaftlicher Bündnispolitik in der Weimarer Republik', in Stegmann *et al.*, *Industrielle Gesellschaft und politisches System*, pp. 259–70; idem, *Landwirtschaftliche Interessen und Demokratie. Ländliche Gesellschaft, Agrarverbände und Staat 1890–1925* (Bonn, 1978), p. 252 ff.; D. Gessner, *Agrarverbände in der Weimarer Republik. Wirtschaftliche und soziale Voraussetzungen agrarkonservativer Politik vor 1933* (Düsseldorf, 1976), p. 66 ff.

79 See K. H. Pohl, *Weimars Wirtschaft und die Aussenpolitik der Republik 1924–1926. Vom Dawes-Plan zum Internationalen Eisenpakt* (Düsseldorf, 1979) (University of Hamburg diss. 1977).

80 See G. D. Feldman, 'German big business between war and revolution. The origins of the Stinnes-Legien agreement', in G. A. Ritter (ed.) *Entstehung und Wandel der modernen Gesellschaft. Festschrift für Hans Rosenberg zu seinem 65. Geburtstag* (Berlin, 1970).

81 On this nexus, see the important study by Bernd Weisbrod, *Schwerindustrie in der Weimarer Republik. Interessenpolitik zwischen Stabilisierung und Krise* (Wuppertal, 1978); on the 'veto bloc', see pp. 35–6.

82 On the problem in general, see L. Preller, *Sozialpolitik in der Weimarer Republik* (Stuttgart, 1949), reprinted by Athenäum-Droste in 1978. Still important is H. Timm, *Die deutsche Sozialpolitik und der Bruch der grossen Koalition im März 1930* (Düsseldorf, 1952) (Uni. of Hamburg

diss.). See also, more recently, Weisbrod, *Schwerindustrie*, pp. 395 ff., 415 ff.

83   D. Stegmann, 'Die Silverberg-Kontroverse 1926. Unternehmerpolitik zwischen Reform und Restauration', in *Sozialgeschichte heute. Festschrift für Hans Rosenberg* (Göttingen, 1974), p. 594 ff.

84   See C.-D. Krohn, 'Autoritärer Kapitalismus. Wirtschaftskonzeptionen im Übergang von der Weimarer Republik zum Nationalsozialismus', in Stegmann *et al.*, *Industrielle Gesellschaft und politisches System*, pp. 113–30.

85   See W. Jochmann, 'Brünings Deflationspolitik und der Untergang der Weimarer Republik', in Stegmann *et al.*, *Industrielle Gesellschaft und politisches System*, pp. 97–112.

86   See M. Grübler, *Die Spitzenverbände der Wirtschaft und das erste Kabinett Brüning. Vom Ende der Grossen Koalition 1929/30 bis zum Vorabend der Bankenkrise 1931* (Düsseldorf, 1982) (Uni. of Hamburg diss. 1977).

87' See H. A. Winkler, *Mittelstand, Demokratie und Nationalsozialismus. Die politische Entwicklung von Handwerk und Kleinhandel in der Weimarer Republik* (Cologne, 1972).

88   The question is a highly contentious one. See D. Stegmann, 'Zum Verhältnis von Grossindustrie und Nationalsozialismus 1930–1933', *Archiv für Sozialgeschichte*, Vol. 13 (1973), pp. 399–482 (with documents); idem, 'Kapitalismus und Faschismus in Deutschland 1932 bis 1934. Zum Stellenwert der Wirtschaftsprogrammatik der NSDAP im Prozess der "Machtergreifung"', *Abendroth-Forum* (Marburg, 1977), pp. 354–61; idem, 'Kapitalismus und Faschismus in Deutschland 1929–1934. Thesen und Materialien zur Restituierung des Primats der Grossindustrie zwischen Weltwirtschaftskrise und beginnender Rüstungskonjunktur', in *Gesellschaft. Beiträge zur Marx'schen Theorie*, Edition Suhrkamp 806 (Frankfurt, 1976), pp. 11–91 (with documents); idem, 'Antiquierte Personalisierung oder sozioökonomische Faschismustheorie? Eine Antwort auf H. A. Turners Kritik an meinen Thesen zum Verhältnis von Nationalsozialismus und Grossindustrie vor 1933', *Archiv für Sozialgeschichte*, Vol. 17 (1977), pp. 275–96; H. A. Turner, *Faschismus und Kapitalismus in Deutschland. Studien zum Verhältnis zwischen Nationalismus und Wirtschaft* (Göttingen, 1972); idem, 'Grossunternehmertum und Nationalsozialismus 1930–1933. Kritisches und Ergänzendes zu zwei neuen Forschungsbeiträgen', *Historische Zeitschrift*, vol. 221 (1975), pp. 18–68; E. Czichon, *Wer verhalf Hitler zur Macht? Zum Anteil der deutschen Industrie an der Zerstörung der Weimarer Republik* (Cologne, 1967); G. W. F. Hallgarten and J. Radkau, *Deutsche Industrie und Politik von Bismarck bis heute* (Frankfurt and Cologne, 1974); and (recently) V. Hentschel, *Weimars letzte Monate. Hitler und der Untergang der Republik* (Düsseldorf, 1978), which entirely ignores interests and structures and reduces the final phase of the Weimar Republic (or, to be more precise, of the presidential cabinets, for 'Weimar' was already finished in 1930) to the personal intrigue of a handful of actors.

89   See H. A. Winkler, 'Ist unser Land faschistisch? Eine Kritik an linken

Theorien – Viele falsche Begriffe', *Die Zeit*, No. 27 (30.6.1978), p. 14; idem, *Revolution, Staat, Faschismus. Zur Revision des Historischen Materialismus* (Göttingen, 1976).

90 See D. Gessner, *Agrardepression und Präsidialregierungen in Deutschland 1930–1933. Probleme des Agrarprotektionismus am Ende der Weimarer Republik* (Düsseldorf, 1977).

91 Winkler, 'Ist unser Land faschistisch?', p. 14.

92 See W. Wette, 'Ideologien, Propaganda und Innenpolitik als Voraussetzungen nationalsozialistischer Kriegspolitik', in W. Deist, M. Messerschmidt, H.-E. Volkmann and W. Wette (eds) *Das Deutsche Reich und das Zweite Weltkrieg*, Vol. 1: *Ursachen und Voraussetzungen der deutschen Kriegspolitik* (Stuttgart, 1979), p. 76 ff. My thanks are due to Messrs Deist, Messerschmidt, Volkmann and Wette for allowing me to see this work in an earlier, manuscript form.

93 Carsten, *Reichswehr and Politics*, p. 368 ff.

94 Stresemann, in a memorandum drafted for a departmental conference on 13.1.1925 and later sent to the governments of the Reich and the *Länder* (dated 30.1.1925). See *Griff*, 1st and 2nd edns, p. 856. In a speech in the Osnabrück Town Hall in December 1918 he said, 'If we succeed in binding the German Austrians to us, then we shall have the great bloc of 70 million Germans of which it was correctly observed by old Bismarck: here we now stand in the middle of Europe like a giant tree-trunk that every one has to go around'. (During the war, in December 1916, former Chancellor Bülow had made a similar statement: 'Even if we should lose this war we shall yet win the game if we annex Austria.') Cited in A. Thimme, *Gustav Stresemann. Eine politische Biographie zur Geschichte der Weimarer Republik* (Hanover and Frankfurt, 1957), p. 46. In the same source (pp. 105 f., 128): 'Briand's Europe and Stresemann's Europe were mutually exclusive', for each aimed at securing Continental hegemony for his own country; the Briand plan and the German-Austrian customs union were concerned with 'the preservation of French power and the extension of German power respectively'.

95 See H. Molt, *Anschluss-Europaplan-Zollunion. Zwischen Locarnopakt 1925 und Zollunionsplan 1931* (Uni. of Hamburg diss. 1979), indicating the connection between political and economic expansion (with comprehensive bibliography).

96 Akten zur Deutschen Auswärtigen Politik 1918–1945, Series B, 1925–1933 (1966), Vol. 1, First Half-volume, Doc. no. 1: note by Senior Counsellor von Dirksen on a German-Lithuanian customs-union and the proposals of Minister Turycki, strictly confidential, 3.12.1925.

97 See Molt, *Anschluss-Europaplan-Zollunion*; D. Stegmann, '"Mitteleuropa" 1925 bis 1934. Zum Problem der Kontinuität deutscher Aussenhandelspolitik von Stresemann bis Hitler', in Stegmann et al., *Industrielle Gesellschaft und politisches System*, pp. 203–24; R. Frommelt, *Paneuropa oder Mitteleuropa. Einigungsbestrebungen im Kalkül deutscher Wirtschaft und Politik 1925–1933* (Stuttgart, 1977). On the Central European

Economic Association (led by G. von Gothein of the DDP after 1927), see Frommelt, p. 23 ff.; for the manipulation of the German Europa Societies by economic interests and government, see Frommelt, p. 85 ff.

98 Posse, 19.5.1932, from the minutes of an executive meeting of the German section of the Central European Economic Association in Berlin, cited in R. Opitz (ed.), *Europastrategien des deutschen Kapitals 1900–1945* (Cologne, 1977), p. 606 f. (No. 74).

99 C. Duisberg, *Abhandlungen, Vorträge, Reden 1922–1933* (Berlin, 1933), cited in R. Opitz (ed.), *Europastrategien,* p. 581 f.

100 Schlenker, 13.2.1931, in an article in *Der Deutsche Volkswirt*, Vol. 5, 20 (1930–31), p. 637 ff.; idem, in printed report (17.6.1931) on the annual general meeting of the Association of German Iron and Steel Industrialists (Federal Archives, Koblenz, R 13 I–130).

101 See H.-E. Volkmann, 'Die NS-Wirtschaft in Vorbereitung des Krieges', in *Ursachen und Voraussetzungen der deutschen Kriegspolitik*, chapter 1 ('Von der Weltwirtschaft zur Grossraumwirtschaft'), p. 177 ff.

102 Wette, 'Ideologien, Propaganda und Innenpolitik', pp. 40, 41, 43 ff., 46, 55 ff., 58.

103 In the post-1945 preoccupation with the churches' 'resistance' to the religious policy of the 'Third Reich', consciousness of the churches' own share in the disparagement and weakening of the Weimar democracy receded. On the Protestant side, a recent study maintains that 'most of the bishops, ecclesiastical officials, pastors and especially the majority of the laiety in the synods' neglected 'to clearly determine their own responsibility . . .; they should have seized the occasion to face up to their own nationalist, even (in many instances) racist and anti-Semitic past and, in particular, their activities in undermining and discrediting the democratic system of Weimar' (W. Jochmann, 'Zur politischen Orientierung der deutschen Protestanten nach 1945', in H. Alberts and J. Thomsen (eds), *Christen in der Demokratie* (Wuppertal, 1978), p. 177).

104 See G. Ritter, *Friedrich der Grosse* (Heidelberg, 1936), pp. 2, 265 ff.; K. Böhme (from whom a Ritter biography may be expected), 'Gerhard Ritter und die Weimarer Republik', *Quaderni di storia*, vol. 2, no. 4 (1976), pp. 85–112; F. Fischer, 'Der deutsche Protestantismus und die Politik im 19. Jahrhundert', p. 473.

105 On the Ebert-Groener 'pact', see J. W. Wheeler-Bennett, *The Nemesis of Power: The German Army in Politics 1918–1945* (Oxford, 1954), p. 25 ff; E.-O. Schüddekopf, *Das Heer und die Republik. Quellen zur Politik der Reichswehrführung* (Hanover and Frankfurt, 1955), p. 14, especially n. 20; G. A. Craig, *The Politics of the Prussian Army, 1640–1945* (Oxford, 1955), pp. 346–54; W. Sauer, *Das Bündnis Ebert-Groener* (unpublished diss., Berlin 1956); Carsten, *Reichswehr and Politics*, pp. 10–12. Groener allowed the monarchy to fall on 9.11.1918 'because he feared that the officer corps would otherwise be dragged under with it'. According to his memoirs, Groener expected 'through our activity to assure the army and the officer corps of a share in power in the new state; if we managed that,

then in spite of the revolution the best and strongest element of the old Prussia would be salvaged for the new Germany' (cited in Sauer, p. 21).

106 Carsten, *Reichswehr and Politics*, p. 202 ff. Thus Baron von Fritsch, later Army Supreme Commander under Hitler, described President Ebert, his own Commander in Chief, to Stülpnagel on 16.11.1924 as 'a quite one-sided Social Democratic partisan and a thorough swine'.

107 For the memorandum of 6.3.1926, see Hillgruber, 'Militarismus am Ende der Weimarer Republik und im Dritten Reich', in *Grossmachtpolitik und Militarismus im 20. Jahrhundert* (Düsseldorf, 1974), p. 41. On the 1924 lecture, see Deist, 'Die Aufrüstung der Wehrmacht', in *Ursachen und Voraussetzungen der deutschen Kriegspolitik*, Vol. 1.

108 Memoranda of Wandel (29.11.1911) and Moltke (21.12.1912) in *Der Weltkrieg. Kriegsrüstung und Kriegswirtschaft*, published by the Reichsarchiv, appendices to vol. 1 (Berlin, 1930), pp. 132–5, 156–74.

109 On the state secretaries' committee (one from each of the Audit Office, the Defence Ministry and the Treasury, meeting for the first time in the fiscal year 1928) and the Müller government, see Deist, 'Die Aufrüstung der Wehrmacht' and 'Die militärpolitischen Voraussetzungen', in *Das Deutsche Reich und der Zweite Weltkrieg*, vol. 1, part 3, pp. 371 ff., 380.

110 On the 1929 Magdeburg congress and the position of the Reichsbanner ('unanimously opposed to a war of revenge or aggression and solidly behind the defensive policy of the republican parties'), see Wette, 'Ideologien, Propaganda und Innenpolitik', p. 77 ff. On the Prussian government and the frontier defence issue, see Carsten, *Reichswehr and Politics*, p. 350 ff.

111 E. W. Hansen, *Reichswehr und Industrie. Rüstungswirtschaftliche Zusammenarbeit und wirtschaftliche Mobilmachungsvorbereitungen 1923–1932* (Boppard, 1978), especially p. 184 f. on the Reich's take-over of the united steelworks at the insistence of the Reichswehr (Schleicher).

112 On this 'soldierly nationalism', see Wette, 'Ideologien, Propaganda und Innenpolitik', p. 46 ff.

113 On the 'reformers' or 'revolutionaries', see Hillgruber, 'Militarismus', p. 37 f. See also A. Sywottek, *Mobilmachung für den Totalen Krieg. Die propagandistische Vorbereitung der deutschen Bevölkerung auf den Zweiten Weltkrieg* (Düsseldorf, 1976), p. 13 ff.

114 See Wheeler-Bennett, *The Nemesis of Power*, p. 289 ff.; Craig, *Politics of the Prussian Army*, p. 470 ff.; K. D. Bracher, W. Sauer and G. Schulz, *Die nationalsozialistische Machtergreifung*, 2nd edn (Cologne and Opladen, 1962), p. 708 ff.; C. H. Bloch, *Die SA und die Krise des NS-Regimes 1934* (Frankfurt, 1970).

115 See K.-J. Müller, 'Der militärische Widerstand', manuscript of lecture delivered to the Hamburg Congress of German Historians in 1978, p. 5 f. According to Müller, 'Hitler's tactically brilliant slogan of the two pillars – the army and the party – that would henceforth support the regime was tailored to military expectations', namely, that the Reichswehr was to be given an elevated place in this 'entente', in the 'coalition of conservative

nationalist and populist nationalist forces with the leadership of the National Socialist movement, as realized on 30 January 1933 in the Hitler cabinet'. See also Müller, *Das Heer und Hitler. Armee und national-sozialistisches Regime 1933–1940* (Stuttgart, 1969), pp. 35 ff., 88 ff.

116 See Deist, in *Das Deutsche Reich und der Zweite Weltkrieg*, vol. 1, part 3, pp. 465 ff., 468; J. Dülffer, *Weimar, Hitler und die Marine. Reichspolitik und Flottenbau 1920–1939* (Düsseldorf, 1973), p. 370 ff. (for the attempt to build a fleet befitting a world power, 1935–9) and p. 204 ff. (for 1932–5 planning developments, from the 'conversion plan' to the Naval Agreement).

117 See D. Petzina, *Autarkiepolitik im Dritten Reich. Der nationalsozial-istische Vierjahresplan* (Stuttgart, 1968). See also Hallgarten and Radkau, *Deutsche Industrie und Politik*, pp. 227 ff., 281 ff.; Petzina, 'Vier-jahresplan und Rüstungspolitik', in F. Forstmeier and H.-E. Volkmann (eds), *Wirtschaft und Rüstung am Vorabend des Zweiten Weltkrieges* (Düsseldorf, 1975).

118 For the 'high degree of concurrence' between Hitler and the military leaders, see Hillgruber, 'Militarismus', p. 49, and idem (on the campaign plans and prognoses of the military chiefs in the Armed Forces High Command and the Army High Command (OKW and OKH)), 'Das Russlandbild der führenden deutschen Militärs vor Beginn des Angriffs auf die Sowjetunion', in A. Fischer, G. Moltmann and K. Schwabe (eds), *Russland, Deutschland, Amerika. Festschrift für Fritz T. Epstein* (Wies-baden, 1978), p. 296 ff.

119 See W. A. Boelcke (ed.), *Deutschlands Rüstung im Zweiten Weltkrieg. Hitlers Konferenzen mit A. Speer 1942–1945* (Frankfurt, 1969).

120 A. Dallin, *German Rule in Russia, 1941–1945* (London, 1957).

121 See H. Winkel, 'Die "Ausbeutung" des besetzten Frankreich', and W. Dlugoborski and C. Madajczyk, 'Ausbeutungssysteme in den besetzten Gebieten Polens und der UdSSR', in F. Forstmeier and H.-E. Volkmann (eds), *Kriegswirtschaft und Rüstung 1939–1945* (Düssel-dorf, 1977), pp. 333 ff. and 375 ff. respectively.

122 See 'Conclusion', *Das Deutsche Reich und der Zweite Weltkrieg*, Vol. 1: *Ursachen und Voraussetzungen der deutschen Kriegspolitik*, pp. 703 ff., 715.

Index

For Product Safety Concerns and Information please contact our EU
representative GPSR@taylorandfrancis.com
Taylor & Francis Verlag GmbH, Kaufingerstraße 24, 80331 München, Germany